Robert C. Sands

Jan. 18. 1911.

T5-ANW-273

"Great Writers."

EDITED BY

ERIC S. ROBERTSON, M.A.,

PROFESSOR OF ENGLISH LITERATURE AND PHILOSOPHY IN THE
UNIVERSITY OF THE PUNJAB, LAHORE.

LIFE OF COLERIDGE.

LIFE

OF

SAMUEL TAYLOR COLERIDGE

BY

HALL CAINE

GEN. THEO. SEMINARY

NEW YORK

LONDON

WALTER SCOTT

24 WARWICK LANE, PATERNOSTER ROW

1887

105225

92
C676ca

GEN THEO. SEMINARY
LIBRARY
NEW YORK

NOTE.

THIS short biography has been compiled from many sources that cannot be mentioned here—table-talk, letters, diaries, memoirs, reminiscences, magazine articles, newspaper reports, and a few documents which have not hitherto been employed by any biographer of Coleridge. To two living Coleridgeans I must more particularly acknowledge my indebtedness—Mr. T. Ashe, and Mr. H. D. Traill. I have, however, been compelled to depart from these excellent authorities in my rendering of certain incidents of the first importance, and in my general reading of Coleridge's character as a man.

CONTENTS.

CHAPTER I.

CHAPTER II.

CHAPTER III.

CHAPTER IV.

CHAPTER V.

CHAPTER VI.

CHAPTER VII.

CHAPTER VIII.

Coleridge physics himself, and unconsciously takes to opium ; goes to Malta (April, 1804) chiefly for his health ; appointed secretary to the governor ; visits Rome ; leaves Rome for England August, 1806 ; a bad correspondent while away, and on bad terms with Southey and his own family on his

CHAPTER IX.

CHAPTER X.

CHAPTER XI.

LIFE OF SAMUEL TAYLOR COLERIDGE.

CHAPTER I.

"I AM grieved," said Southey, "that you never met Coleridge. All other men whom I have ever known are mere children to him, and yet all is palsied by a total want of moral strength." "He is like a lump of coal rich with gas," said Scott, "which lies expending itself in puffs and gleams, unless some shrewd body will clap it into a cast-iron box, and compel the compressed element to do itself justice." "He is the only person I ever knew, who answered to the idea of a man of genius," said Hazlitt; "he is the only person from whom I ever learnt anything. His genius had . . . angelic wings, and fed on manna. He talked on for ever; and you wished him to talk on for ever." "He is," said De Quincey, "the largest and most spacious intellect, the subtlest and most comprehensive that has yet existed among men." "Impiety to Shakespeare!" cried Landor; "treason to Milton! I give up all the rest, even Bacon. Certainly, since their day we have had nothing at all comparable with him. Byron and Scott were but as gun-flints to a granite mountain; Wordsworth has one angle of resemblance."

Samuel Taylor Coleridge was born on October 21, 1772, at Ottery St. Mary, in Devonshire. His father combined the functions of vicar and schoolmaster of his native parish. The vicar had been twice married, and Samuel was the youngest of thirteen children. His mother is described as a homely, house-minding, unimaginative woman, uneducated, out of sympathy with the accomplishments that were fashionable among ladies, resembling Martha in being over careful in many things. Her husband appears to have been a man of simple manners and amiable character, a little eccentric, a little pedantic, a little unmindful of immediate interests. Coleridge used to tell a story which he considered characteristic of both his parents. On one occasion the old gentleman had to take a journey which would keep him from home three or four days. His wife packed his little trunk, and impressed upon him the necessity of putting on a clean shirt every day. He gave the required promise, and set out. On his return it was observed that he had not lost flesh during his absence. In due course his trunk was unpacked, and then it was discovered that all the linen had disappeared. The good man had strictly obeyed his wife's instructions by putting on a clean shirt every day, but had always forgotten to take off the old one. It seems to have been a constant habit of this rural clergyman to diversify his discourses with liberal quotations from the Hebrew, which he described as " the immediate language of the Holy Ghost." His rustic flock appear to have acquired a mysterious reverence for this kind of teaching, and when the old vicar was gone, they thought lightly of a successor from whom no "immediate language" was ever heard. Recalling the half-conscious pedantry, and less than half-conscious eccentricity, of thi· gentle, learned, simple-hearted father, Coleridge would compare him with Parson Adams. The comparison was meant in reverence and deep love, and it serves as a key to one side of the poet's own character. In gentleness, in unselfishness in "other-worldliness," and even in an amusing indifference to some of the plain issues of life, the vicar and schoolmaster of Ottery St. Mary was not more like Fielding's immortal character than he was like his own famous son.

"I was the last child," says Coleridge, "the youngest of ten by the same mother, that is to say, John, William (who died in infancy), James, William, Edward, George, Luke, Ann, Francis, and myself, Samuel Taylor Coleridge, beneficially abridged Esteese (Εστησε), *i.e.*, S.T.C., and the thirteenth, taking in three sisters by my dear father's first wife—Mary, afterwards Mrs. Bradley ; Sarah, who married a seaman, and is lately dead ; and Elizabeth, afterwards Mrs. Phillips, who alone was bred up with us after my birth, and whom alone of the three I was wont to think of as a sister, though not exactly, yet I did not know why, the same sort of sister as my sister Nancy." Before Coleridge came of age, death had made many gaps in this list—five brothers and one sister (the only daughter of his mother) were lost to him. He was delicate as a child, self-absorbed and even morbidly imaginative. There is a story that in his fifth or sixth year, having quarrelled with his brother, and being in dread of a whipping, he stole

away from home and spent the whole of an October night
of rain and wind on the banks of the Otter, where he was
found at daybreak perished with cold, and without the
power of using his limbs. Thrice in later life he disappeared as mysteriously, and in each case he seems to have
been under the same morbid impulse. " Alas ! I had,"
he says, "all the simplicity, all the docility of the little
child, but none of the child's habits. I never thought as
a child ; never had the language of a child." He was first
educated under his father at the Free Grammar School,
and displayed some precocity. Before he had completed
his ninth year the old vicar died. " My most dear, my
most revered father died suddenly," he says. "O that I
might so pass away if I, like him, were an Israelite without guile." A few months after the vicar's death,
Coleridge was removed, his widowed mother being poor,
to the house of a maternal uncle in London. His connection with his native place was then practically at an
end. He returned to it in manhood on short visits to
one of his brothers, but his interests from his tenth year
onwards lay elsewhere. His memory continued to revolve
about it very fondly, but his native county had taken
more hold of his imagination than of his affections. In
one place, he speaks of himself as " transplanted " before
his " soul had fixed its first domestic loves," and as a
stranger in his own home and birth-place. In another
place, he describes his home-sickness when at school in
after years ; his day-dreams of the old church tower,
whose bells haunted him even under the preceptor's stern
gaze, when his eyes were fixed in mock study on his
swimming book. And in yet another place, he says that

so deeply impressed upon his mind are the scenes of his childhood that he can never close his eyes in the sun without seeing afresh the waters of the Otter, its willowy banks, the plank that crossed it, and the sand of varied tints that lay in its bed.

> " Visions of childhood ! oft have ye beguiled
> Lone manhood's cares, yet waking fondest sighs ;
> Ah ! that once more I were a careless child."

That his affections were not very closely bound up with his birth-place is sufficiently seen in the fact that, though "most a stranger, most with naked heart," at Ottery St. Mary, his mother continued to reside there, having made her home in the family of his brother George, who succeeded his father in the double office of vicar and schoolmaster. It is curious that Coleridge alludes to his mother but rarely. I cannot recall an instance of his active interest in her welfare. He seems to have been content to envy his brother the joy of seeing his tottering little ones embracing the aged knees, and climbing the lap at which he lisped his first brief prayer. It is barely conceivable that a boy removed from home in his tenth year is "transplanted" too early to allow his soul to fix the first of all domestic loves.

Coleridge remained three months at the house of his uncle in London, and was then admitted, through the influence of one of his father's old pupils, to Christ's Hospital. A vivid picture of the great charity school as it existed at this period, July, 1782, has been drawn by one of its most famous pupils. The hardships which the boys underwent must have been grievous enough. At all

events, Coleridge indulged in later life many pathetic
reminiscences of the wretchedness of his school-days.
He thought himself ill-conditioned as to material comforts,
and quite out of the range of that sympathy of which a
shy, sensitive child of an affectionate disposition stands
in need. It was one of the regulations of the school
that an entire holiday, or leave-day, should be given at
intervals. This was a privilege to such of the boys as had
friends living in London ; but it was often a punishment
to such as had no friends there. Whatever the weather
might be on the periodical leave-day, the gates of the
school were closed on every pupil from early morning
until sunset. Coleridge was homeless, and, according to
his own account, friendless in London, and these holidays
were not unmixed blessings to him. In fine weather he
would indulge the one athletic pleasure in which he had
any skill, that of swimming, in the New River. In wet
weather he would tramp round and round the Newgate
market, waiting for the school gates to re-open. There is
reason to think that at this time he had somewhat outgrown
the delicate health of his very early boyhood, but he was
still a child, and entirely cut off from home associations. It
would be folly to suppose that when in after-life he spoke
of his wretchedness at Christ's Hospital as a shy, shrinking
boy, exposed to many discomforts and out of the range of
solace, he drew a fancy picture. Pleasures of many kinds
he no doubt enjoyed. His temperament was naturally
joyous, and above all else it was affectionate. He was a
creature made to love and to be beloved. Though
distinctly the reverse of a boyish boy, though fonder of
books than of play, though prone to indulge the medita-

tive tendency to a degree that boys do not usually consider heroic, Coleridge must have been a boy that other boys would like. He was fond of solitude, but he was sociable too. There was healthy humour, and, in a less dubious sense than that of the friend who said so, there was a good deal of fun in Coleridge. He must have been a likeable lad, and that implies that he must have been to some extent a happy one. But there ought to be no hesitation in accepting his assurance that, on the whole, Christ's Hospital was a sufficiently stern home for an orphan boy of ten.

He remained between eight and nine years at school, and during that period he never entirely conquered his loneliness, and his yearning for some sort of home. Five years after leaving Ottery, he made the acquaintance, while rambling through the city on his enforced leave-day, of a shoemaker and his wife, and the good people showed the boy some kindness. This suggested to him the idea of being apprenticed to shoemaking, and so fixed was the lad's intention that the honest shoemaker called on the master to make the necessary arrangements. It is probable that Coleridge was willing to desert Christ's Hospital in favour of the shoemaker's home without any sanction from authority. Although it was customary to put the boys to trades as opportunities arose, Coleridge's request was not granted. The master got into a great rage, knocked the lad down, and pushed the shoemaker out of the room. In reference to the circumstance the poet afterwards said, " I lost the opportunity of supplying safeguards to the *understandings* of those who, perhaps, will never thank me for what I am aiming to do in exercising their *reason*." Curiously

enough, his mind reverted to this idea years afterwards,
when, thanking God for His dispensations, and believing
them to be the best possible, he ventured the conjecture that he might have been yet more thankful if
it had pleased Providence to make him a journeyman
shoemaker instead of an author by trade. During the
closing years of his life at school the craving for domestic
love was no less strong. He made the acquaintance of a
widow lady whose son he, as an upper boy, had protected,
and he speaks of her with affection as one who taught
him what it was to have a mother. He loved her as
a son. She had three daughters, and perhaps it would
be a little rash to say that the same desire to escape
from his solitariness prompted him to fall in love with
the eldest. The calf-love was not without ardour and
the qualities that last. " Oh, from sixteen to nineteen,"
he says, "what hours of Paradise had Allen and I in
escorting the Miss Evanses home on a Saturday, who were
then at a milliner's, whom we used to think, and who I
believe really was, such a nice lady ;—and we used to
carry thither, of a summer morning, the pillage of the
flower gardens within six miles from town, with sonnet
or love rhymes wrapped round the nosegay." He met
his young milliner some years afterwards in Wrexham.
"She gave a short, sharp cry," he says, "almost a shriek ;
. . . sickened and well-nigh fainted. . . . God bless
her !" Thus Coleridge's friendlessness in London was
not entirely unbroken by strange attachments, and it is
sufficiently obvious that his timidity and sensitiveness were
not so acute that they forbade on occasion even the
pillage of the flower gardens.

His brother Luke came up to London to walk the hospitals, and it would appear that the young surgeon did not neglect him. Every Saturday that the boy could obtain leave from school he trudged away with his brother to the London Hospital. The result was that he became wild to be apprenticed to a surgeon. "Oh the bliss," he says, "if I was permitted to hold the plasters or attend the dressings. . . . English, Latin, yea, Greek books of medicine read I incessantly. Blanchard's 'Latin Medical Dictionary' I had nearly by heart." "It was a wild dream," he says later, but the friend who knew him best in his early manhood took a more serious view of the possibilities. "Nature, who seems to have meant you for half-a-dozen different things when she made you," says Southey in a letter to Coleridge, "meant you for a physician among the rest." Coleridge formed ardent friendships at Christ's Hospital. Middleton, afterwards Bishop of Calcutta, was his first "patron and protector," being some years his senior; and a lifelong friendship, riveted by many ties of sympathy, was there begun with another boy who was three years his junior. This was Charles Lamb, a weakly but pretty boy, with curling black hair, and a Jewish cast of features, thoughtful, timid, sensitive, the son of a barrister's clerk who lived in Crown Office Row. Lamb had a sister ten years older than himself, and she became an important agent not only in his own life, but in that of his friend also.

No schemes, however, for material comfort such as prompted Coleridge to offer himself as apprentice to the shoemaker, no casual dreams of a profession such as suggested surgery as an outlet for his energy, no ardour of

comradeship such as Lamb and Middleton appear to
have excited, could cure a nature like Coleridge's of its
tendency to solitariness.   If he had been more favourably
conditioned as to immediate surroundings, this tendency
might have been fostered with less danger to the
sweetness, the amiability and joyousness of his natural
temperament.   But in the lap of home he must have
been a solitary lad still.   The most illustrious of his
friends describes it in *The Prelude* as a constant habit of
his life, to lie on the leaded roof of the school and look
up at the sky and dream of the trees, the meadows and
the rivers of his native place.   The "shaping spirit of
imagination" was strong upon him in the years of his
long exile as a boy in the streets of the city.   It had
taken hold of him while he was even yet at home, where,
according to his own account, he never played except
by himself, and then only at acting over what he had
been reading or fancying.   He was a poet born.   At
Ottery St. Mary, while still a child, with the docility of
a child, but few of a child's habits, he would prance
along the roads, swinging a stick in his hands, and
imagining himself to be one of the seven champions of
Christendom as he cut down the weeds and nettles that
lay in his path.   When he came up to London, the
poetic impulse was not less strong upon him because the
scene was less romantic.   He read Shakespeare and
Homer and much poetry besides.   As often from poetic
prompting as from the physical impulses natural to a
boy, he swam in the New River.   It must have been at the
demand of some conception of romance, in imitation
perhaps of a feat recorded in poetry, that one day he

swam the river in his clothes. The clothes were allowed
to dry on his back, with the inevitable consequences to
his health. Jaundice and rheumatic fever kept him fully
half the time from seventeen to eighteen years of age in
the sick-ward, and it is possible that chronic effects,
attended by a far graver tragedy, ensued. One day
in the street, wholly self-absorbed, alone among crowds,
deaf to the turmoil about him, he fancied himself
Leander swimming the Hellespont, and thrust out his
arms while buffeting the waves. In doing so, he
unwittingly tugged at the coat-tails of a gentleman, who
at first supposed that the boy was a clumsy young thief
with designs upon his pocket. On learning the truth the
gentleman was so well disposed to encourage Coleridge's
taste for reading that he paid his subscription to a cir-
culating library in Cheapside. This was a high privilege
to the lonely lad. He read voraciously, devouring
literature, it is said, at the rate of two volumes a day.

It was natural that poetry should not be his sole
intellectual food. He read Voltaire and blossomed into
an atheist. When the master of Christ's Hospital refused
to countenance the project of apprenticing Coleridge to
a shoemaker, he advanced the plan of sending him to
the University as the first step towards Holy Orders.
But Coleridge declined to become a clergyman, and in
answer to an inquiry as to his reasons for objecting, he
boldly announced himself as an infidel. The master
was the Rev. James Bowyer, a very sensible, but a very
severe man, who believed in the efficacy of the birch, and
had the courage of his convictions. "So, sirrah, you
are an infidel are you?" he said; "then I'll flog your

infidelity out of you!" And without more ado he proceeded to exterminate Voltaire by force of a flogging,
which Coleridge feelingly described as sound if not salu-
tary. The study of theology gave way to a rage for
metaphysics, occasioned in the first instance by the
essays on Liberty and Necessity in Cato's "Letters."
"Even before my fifteenth year," he says, alluding to the
period of the shoemaking project, "I had bewildered
myself in metaphysics. Nothing else pleased me. History . . . lost all interest in my mind. Poetry itself,
yea, novels and romances, became insipid to me." In
his friendless wanderings through London on leave-days
he was delighted if any passenger, "especially if he were
dressed in black," would enter into conversation with
him. Then he would soon find the means of directing
the talk to his favourite subjects. The craze for metaphysics lasted some two or three years, and then left "a
blessed interval" of some twelve years. When no longer
tortured by abstruse researches, his natural faculty, his
imagination, was allowed to expand, and his natural
tendency, his love of nature and the sense of beauty, to
develop itself without restraint.

The severe teacher who flogged him out of his infidelity ridiculed him out of false taste in poetry. In the
English compositions of his pupils, the Rev. Mr. Bowyer
showed no mercy to phrase, metaphor, or image, un-
supported by sound sense. "Harp? harp? lyre? Pen
and ink, boy, you mean! Muse, boy, muse? Your
nurse's daughter you mean! Pierian springs? Oh aye,
the cloister-pump, I suppose!" The sense of obligation
to this master seems never to have grown dim in Cole-

ridge's mind; but the sense of his severities appears to have been no less vivid. Long afterwards the painful sensations of his rigid rule had left impressions that were deep enough to give his pupil many a distempered sleep furnished by dreams of the stern days of boyhood. It shows the nature of Coleridge's feelings towards the master of Christ's Hospital, that, when Bowyer died, as late as 1814, Charles Lamb wrote: "Old Jimmy Bowyer dead at last. Lay thy animosity against Jimmy in the grave. Do not *entail* it on posterity." Among other intellectual obligations which Coleridge lay under to his master must certainly be counted that of preparing him for the appreciation of poetry that was both natural and full of nature. To such poetry his mind had, as we have seen, a congenial tendency. His passion for romance was deep, but his love of simple nature was even deeper. The boy who lay on the leaded roof of the schoolhouse to gaze at the clouds and dream of the beauty of Ottery St. Mary, was hardly likely to be content with "that school of French poetry, condensed and invigorated by English understanding," in which the highest merit was "just and acute observations on men and manners in an artificial state of society . . . conveyed in smooth and strong epigrammatic couplets." Mr. Bowyer favoured the natural tendency toward nature, and then a more potent influence finally determined it. In 1789, when Coleridge was eighteen, a little pamphlet of fourteen sonnets was published by William Lisle Bowles. The booklet was sent to Coleridge by his old schoolfellow, Middleton, then at Cambridge. It came to him as a revelation of real, dignified and harmonious poetry. He was not then acquainted with what Cowper had done in the same direction, and it is possible that Burns's transcripts from nature were equally unknown to him. Recognizing in Bowles's poetry rebellion against established canons of poetry, he laboured to make proselytes to the improved taste and judgment, of all with whom he conversed. Too poor to purchase copies of the pamphlet, he made within a year no fewer than forty manuscript transcripts, as the best presents he could offer to those who had won his regard. When he came to write his literary life a quarter of a century later, he adopted a somewhat apologetic tone as to this boyish enthusiasm. "The reader," he says, "must make himself acquainted with the general style of composition that was at that time deemed poetry, in order to understand and account for the effect produced upon me by the sonnets, 'The Monody at Matlock' and the 'Hope' of Mr. Bowles; for it is peculiar to original genius to become less and less striking, in proportion to its success in improving the taste and judgment of its contemporaries." The apology is unnecessary. Bowles was not a great poet, but he was a true one. The young poet at Christ's Hospital recognized the genuine note when he heard it, though the voice that sounded it was the reverse of strong or of good compass. By and by another voice of higher quality sounded the same harmonious note, and then Coleridge was justified of his enthusiasm.

The "blessed interval" produced fruit after its kind, and Coleridge wrote poetry. Some of it was whimsical, such as the song of "The Nose;" some of it very sentimental, such as "Genevieve" and the "First Advent of

Love ; " some of it purely scholastic, such as the two translations from Catullus ; none of it was of the smallest consequence. Probably much of his early verse has deservedly perished. Coleridge remained at Christ's Hospital until the autumn of 1790, having lived there a little more than eight years, and being then almost eighteen years of age. His friend Lamb, though three years his junior, was already a year gone from school, and was now a clerk in the South Sea House. Coleridge's personal appearance as a schoolboy has been repeatedly described. In one account he is presented as "tall and striking, and with long black hair ; " in another account we see him as he appeared in play hours walking to and fro with a book in hand, or sitting on a doorstep, his breeches unbuttoned at the knees, and his shoes down at the heels. It is hardly conceivable that he was a comely lad. Flabby cheeks and heavy lips would sufficiently disturb the effect of large and beautiful eyes, and a winning smile. There is a tradition that Bowyer sometimes gave him an extra stripe of the birch "because he was so ugly." The one vital portrait which we possess is by Lamb, and, familiar as it is, must be quoted here : " Come back into memory, like as thou wert in the day-spring of thy fancies, with hope like a fiery column before thee—the dark pillar not yet turned—Samuel Taylor Coleridge—Logician, Metaphysician, Bard !—How have I seen the casual passer through the cloisters stand still, entranced with admiration (while he weighed the dispro-portion between the *speech* and the *garb* of the young Mirandula) to hear thee unfold in thy deep and sweet intonations, the mysteries of Jamblichus, or Plotinus (for

even in those years thou waxedst not pale at such philosophic draughts), or reciting Homer in his Greek, or
Pindar—while the walls of the old Grey Friars re-echoed
to the accents of *the inspired charity-boy !*"

In quoting this apostrophy it is only necessary to say
that there must indeed have been a good deal of fun in
the young Mirandula, or else in the casual passer through
the cloisters, in Lamb or in his schoolfellows.

CHAPTER II.

O N leaving Christ's Hospital Coleridge appears to have taken the natural step of running down to Devonshire to see his mother and brothers. What occurred there is not yet known, but there seems to be reason to believe that the family relations were afterwards somewhat strained. He must have been quite penniless, and he was probably without any clear designs as to his future; but after six or seven months he was entered at Jesus College, Cambridge, as a student sent up by Christ's Hospital. This was in February, 1791. Whether he had Holy Orders or college honours and a college life in view is uncertain. His University career is almost a blank. We know that at Cambridge he rejoined his schoolfellow Middleton, and read with him, and that in 1792 he gained the gold medal for a Greek ode. This argues some assiduity at the outset, but it would appear that after the new broom had grown old it ceased to sweep clean. Middleton left Cambridge in due course, and then Coleridge's studies became desultory and intermittent. We gather that the comparative freedom of life at the University was not entirely favourable to the strictly academical studies of such a young man as Coleridge. He was, as we have seen, a

great talker, and as such he most of all loved social con-
verse. His rooms at college became a centre of attraction.
He was an enthusiast, and other enthusiasts found in
him a rallying point. They talked religion, poetry,
philosophy, and, above all, politics. The air was full of
many noises just then, and there were subjects enough,
from Mirabeau to Priestley, and from Pitt to Robespierre,
to content the hearts of the politicians and theologians in
embryo. Coleridge's feelings and imagination could not
remain unkindled. His sympathies were with the democracy in the great struggle for political regeneration that
was going on in Europe. He was enthusiastic for France
and the Revolution; but he was never a Jacobin. His
brother James used to say, " No, Samuel is no Jacobin;
he is a hot-headed Moravian." There is a tradition that
on one occasion he planned with an undergraduate, who
afterwards became a Lord Chancellor, the democratic
trick of laying on one of the college lawns a train of
gunpowder, which, when fired, exhibited in the singed
grass the words " Liberty and Equality." The story is
the reverse of Coleridgean; but more in harmony with
his character is the anecdote of his behaviour at the trial
of Frend, a fellow of Jesus College, for defamation of the
Church of England in printing certain opinions founded
on Unitarian doctrine. At some observation made by
one of Frend's defenders, Coleridge is said to have
clapped his hands, and this indecorum was immediately
challenged by a proctor who charged it upon a student
sitting next to Coleridge. " 'Twas you, sir," said the
proctor in a loud voice. " Would, sir, that I had the
power," answered the student, and he held up the stump

of a right arm. Afterwards Coleridge went to the proctor and confessed that it was he who had clapped his hands. "I know that well. You have had a narrow escape," was the answer. Coleridge appears to have had distinct leanings towards Unitarian doctrine in these early years at Cambridge, and this circumstance sufficiently shows that the idea of going into the Church did not enter largely into his calculations.

The vacation of 1793 was spent by Coleridge in his native place. He seems to have been reasonably happy there, and to have made some excursions in pleasant company. It would not be true to say that the strained relations with his own people were at all modified by this visit. Rarely in later years did he show an active interest in his family ; rarely did he exchange a letter with any of his relatives. He spoke of himself as grievously wounded. His sensibilities had been outraged—how or why may presently be explained. A poem which he addressed to his brother three years afterwards was something less than a spontaneous tribute of affection, but its reflections on his own domestic isolation were none the less sincere. To touch this old wound is hardly necessary, especially as we are unable to do so with any certainty of hand. But a little light in this dark place would help us to understand Coleridge better than we do. Perhaps his family contributed some little to the expense of sending him to the University, and perhaps he seemed guilty of the ingratitude of throwing away in Unitarianism the substantial rewards for which they had sacrificed themselves. There was a more obvious breach, and this shall soon appear.

Notwithstanding the delights of literary reunions at his rooms, despite the ardour of political partisanship and the enthusiasm of poetic idolatry, with all that these bring when life is young and hope is strong, and the dark pillar has not yet turned, Coleridge's life at Cambridge was not a happy one. He was in debt, and no doubt this preyed upon him. At one time he spoke of his debts as something less than a hundred pounds. The sum was not prodigious, but it was enough, and tradition tells how he contracted the obligation. When he took possession of his rooms an upholsterer waited upon him and offered to furnish them. Coleridge mistook him for an official of the college, and when asked how he should like the furnishing done, answered, "Just as you please, sir." Perhaps this was an act of astounding unwisdom in a young gentlemen of eighteen years and a half. Perhaps it was a pardonable misadventure. At all events, it involved Coleridge in a debt of something like the sum mentioned. The story is not necessary to account for the circumstance that the orphan son of a poor clergyman was tormented by monetary difficulties. Whether debt was Coleridge's sole trouble, or whether his affectionate nature was ill at ease from the family estrangement already referred to, or whether, in truth, his affections were yet more deeply involved in painful memories of the young milliner or any other person likely to give rise to chagrin at disappointment in love, the end of many "viper thoughts" was something unexpected. In December, 1793, Coleridge was missing from Cambridge, and all inquiries as to his whereabouts were for a time quite fruitless. This was the second of several mysterious disappearances which it will be necessary to chronicle in traversing his life. What had now become of Coleridge? He had fled to London. With little money in his purse, and in no mood to indulge ordinary comforts, he began his career there by spending a whole night on a door-step in Chancery Lane. To the beggars who accosted even him in his desolation he emptied his slender purse.

Next morning he enlisted in a regiment of dragoons. He gave the name of Silas Titus Comberbach, which represented at least his own initials. Probably he made the most awkward member of the awkward squad. His horsemanship was so bad that he thought his horse would sympathize with his cognomen. He made a poor dragoon, but a good messmate. At cleaning his horse and accoutrements his abilities were not conspicuous, but he was a past-master at telling stories in the mess-room, at writing love-letters for his illiterate comrades, and at nursing the sick in the hospital. Hence he was a favourite in the regiment. Four months passed, the regiment was stationed at Reading, and the missing undergraduate remained a tolerably happy dragoon. But the thought of wasted opportunities and of hopes defeated was not to be put away. With a piece of chalk Coleridge wrote on his stall a Latin legend which means that he is doubly wretched who has once been happy. This bit of scholarship betrayed him. An officer chanced to see the legend, and learning that Coleridge was the writer he made him his orderly. It was part of Cole-ridge's new function to walk behind his officer in the streets. At this duty he was one day recognized by a student from the University, and the end of it all was that

Coleridge's friends procured his discharge. He had joined the regiment at Reading on December 3, 1793; he left it at Hounslow on April 4, 1794.

Stories are current to show that this rather silly episode was the result of a period of dissipation. The idea of enlistment is said to have been suggested to Coleridge by the casual sight of a poster announcing that a "few smart lads" were wanted for the "15th Elliot's Light Dragoons;" and the impulse to enlistment is said to have been nothing more serious than the reflection that he had all his life had "a violent antipathy to soldiers and horses," and that "the sooner he cured himself of these absurd prejudices the better." This is needless, and perhaps offensive trifling. The episode is an exhibition of weakness and folly at the best; let us not go out of our way to make it an exhibition of debauchery and idiocy also. It may be that in certain poems Coleridge appears to favour the notion that dissipation played a part in the unaccountable misadventure, and it is certain that the incident could be intelligible to the minds of some of his acquaintances only in the light of excess. But in solemn moods Coleridge was wont to repudiate the immoralities that his family, among others, laid to his charge in this connection. "Were I," he says, "to fix on that week of my existence on which my moral being would have presented to a pitying guardian angel the most interesting spectacle, it would be that very week in London in which I was believed by my family to have abandoned myself to debauchery of all kinds, and *thus* to have involved myself in disreputable pecuniary embarrassments." Obviously the debts were at the root of the family difference, and the groundless accusations of the folk at Ottery St. Mary were calculated to widen the breach. Coleridge's spirit never humbled itself in this regard. His sensibilities had indeed been grievously wounded. He may have known "just so much of folly" as made maturer years "more wise." More probably he was of a nature untroubled by sensual temptations. He never entirely forgave the mistake of his family. No importunities could prevail with him to go back and join hands. He stood aside proudly, letting his heart bleed at the thought that he was most a stranger in his native place, where his brother's children climbed his mother's knee. It has been worth while to dwell on this estrangement. Without a proper sense of its importance in the record of Coleridge's early manhood, much of his subsequent depression of soul seems to be no better than a conscious attempt to suck the eggs of melancholy.

CHAPTER III.

COLERIDGE returned to Cambridge. He does not appear to have borne himself after his ludicrous misadventure like a creature with its tail between its legs. A poet who would have been grateful if Providence had made him a shoemaker, could not be humbled by the reflection that fate had nearly made him a soldier. Save for the wound it brought to his affections, his brief career as a dragoon was almost as much lost to his consciousness as if it had never been. On the life of such a man as Bunyan or Burns it must have left an impression that nothing could remove. The sympathies of Coleridge were all but untouched by it. Coleridge lived in a world apart wherein such an incident was little more than a passing accident. The realities of life were at all times less real to him than the workings of the mind. He was soon immersed in fresh forms of intellectual activity.

Towards the middle of 1793 Coleridge met with Wordsworth's first publication, "Descriptive Sketches," then newly issued. The old admiration of Bowles was now in large part transferred to Wordsworth. "Seldom, if ever," says Coleridge, "was the emergence of an original poetic genius above the literary horizon more

evidently announced." This ardour of discipleship was
to bear fruit in the future, but meantime another accident was to lead to immediate issues. It will be remembered that the schoolfellow with whom Coleridge at
sixteen spent the "hours of Paradise" in escorting the
young milliners home on Saturday nights, after "pillaging
the flower gardens within six miles from town," was a
kindred sad soul named Allen. Now when Allen left
Christ's Hospital he went to Oxford, and thither Coleridge, in his last year at Cambridge, made his way on
a visit to the companion of former days. One of Allen's
friends at Oxford was Southey, and naturally enough
Coleridge and Southey met. Robert Southey was a
Bristol man two years Coleridge's junior. He was a
notable person at the University. His views were
heterodox as to theology, and republican as to politics,
and he was a poet with sympathies at one with the new
school of Cowper. He had been expelled from Westminster for writing in *The Flagellant* an article against
flogging, and by reason of that disgrace he had been
refused admission at Christ's Church. Balliol had taken
him, and when Coleridge and he came together he
was an undergraduate who dared to appear in hall with
unpowdered wig. The meeting was auspicious. It was
like the magnet to the steel, or, say, tinder to the match.
These inflamed spirits lost no time in setting each other
afire. "Allen is with us daily," writes Southey, "and
his friend from Cambridge, Coleridge. . . . He is of
most uncommon merit—of the strongest genius, the
clearest judgment, the best heart." This is sufficiently
indicative of the way the wind blew, but a bigger straw

was soon sent adrift from the other side   Coleridge
started with a party of friends on a pleasure tour in Wales,
and on the way he wrote this first letter to Southey at
Oxford : "You are averse to gratitudinarian flourishes,
else would I talk about hospitality, attention, etc., etc. ;
however, as I must not thank you, I will thank my stars.
Verily, Southey, I like not Oxford, nor the inhabitants
of it.   I would say thou art a nightingale among owls ;
but thou art so songless and heavy towards night that I
will rather liken thee to the matin lark ; thy *nest* is in a
blighted cornfield, where the sleepy poppy nods its red-
cowled head, and the weak-eyed mole plies his dark
work ; but thy soaring is even unto heaven.   Or let me
add (my appetite for similes is truly canine at this
moment) that as the Italian nobles their new-fashioned
doors, so thou must make the adamantine gate of
Democracy turn on its golden hinges to most sweet
music."   Southey loved the blighted cornfield of Oxford
as little as Coleridge ; that matin lark thought so ill of
Oxford's cowl-headed poppies and weak-eyed moles that
it did not trouble to sing to them.   Southey left abruptly
without waiting for his degree.   The long vacation commenced soon after Coleridge's departure for Wales, and
Southey went down to visit an aunt at Bath.   Coleridge
returned by Bristol, and there the new friends clasped
fraternal hands again.

There were many persons at Bristol with whom the
young poets found themselves in sympathy.   Foremost
among these were a family of young ladies, the daughters
of Stephen Fricker, lately dead, who had carried on a
manufactory of sugar-pans at Westbury, and had fallen

into difficulties, and left a widow and six children wholly
unprovided for.   Southey was engaged to one of the
Misses Fricker, and a young friend named Robert
Lovell was already married to another of them.   The
eldest of the young ladies was Sarah, then twenty-three
years of age, and hitherto unappropriated.   Coleridge
promptly fell in love with her.   The ladies were all
comely and all religious, and one of them, the fitting
one, appears to have been in trouble for the unorthodox
soul of Southey.   Robert Lovell was a Quaker, a poet,
and a thoroughly good fellow.   He attached himself to
Coleridge as he had previously attached himself to
Southey, but for a short time a cloud hung over their
friendship.   This was when Coleridge conceived the
idea that Lovell was not promoting his union with Sarah.
Then they met without speaking, and passed as strangers.
Matters came to a crisis, and Coleridge exclaimed,
" Lovell ! you are a villain ! "   " Oh, you are quite mis-
taken," said a friend, a bookseller, " Lovell is proud in the
hope of having you for a brother-in-law, and only wishes
you from prudential motives to delay your union."   This
was a possibility which had escaped Coleridge's observation, but it commended itself to his intelligence, and
in a few days he and Lovell were as sociable as ever.
The bookseller was Joseph Cottle, a year older than
Coleridge, in business in Bristol, having a taste for literature, and some manuscript poems lying snugly in the
drawer.   Cottle turned out a useful acquaintance, and
he was so far a man of reading and culture that the
relation between him and the young poets from the
universities was that of valued friendship.   Southey had

brought with him from Oxford a young man of twenty, of fair abilities and amiable disposition, the son of a Somersetshire farmer, who intended him for the Church. This was George Burnet, destined to play a subordinate part in a forthcoming farce, and not altogether to play it with acceptance. Burnet followed the lead of Lovell, Southey, and Coleridge by proposing for Martha, a fourth daughter of the house of the Frickers ; but the lady rejected him on the ground that, unlike her sisters, she did not choose to be made a wife in a hurry. She was permitted to abide by her resolution, and died a maid at seventy-three. The circle of literary people who found a rallying-point at Bristol, when Coleridge and Southey arrived there in 1794, included some notable names. There were Hannah More, whom Southey saw at Barley Wood ; Robert Hall, the Baptist preacher ; Ann Yearsley, the literary milkwoman ; and William Gilbert, the inspired and deranged author of the " Hurricane," a poem which contains some exquisite passages of poetry accompanied by yet more noble passages of prose. The group was a goodly one of men and women living the intellectual life. Coleridge and Southey found the atmosphere congenial. Their presence in Bristol was a subject of interest. Lovell, being a Bristol man, introduced his friends to the Bristol people. " Never," says Cottle, " will the effect be effaced produced on me by Southey. Tall, dignified, possessing great suavity of manners ; an eye piercing, with a countenance full of genius, kindliness, and intelligence." Coleridge produced an impression no less favourable. " I instantly descried his intellectual character," says the bookseller, " exhibiting as he did an eye, a brow, and a forehead indicative of commanding genius."

The poets wrote a poem together, "The Fall of Robespierre;" but even poetry paled in interest before a socialist scheme which they now set afoot. Southey and Burnet at Oxford had talked over the tyrannical wickedness of the existing order of society, until they had conceived of a plan by which the coil of injustice was to be unravelled.[1] This was the rather simple device of a community of persons settling in America on some spot that should be quite outside the range of governments, and therefore untroubled by laws and taxes. When Coleridge came up on his visit to Allen, he embraced the scheme of Southey and Allen, and gave it the help of his philosophic mind in formulating it into a political system. Forthwith the system came to be known as Pantisocrasy, and its aim as Aspheterism. Pantisocrasy meant the equal government of all; and Aspheterism meant the generalization of individual property. These two were to do the civilized world some general service, but they were especially welcome for the particular service they were to do the persons who discovered them. Southey writes to his brother, "You are unpleasantly situated, so is my mother; so were we all until this grand scheme of Pantisocrasy flashed upon our minds, and now all is perfectly delightful." Coleridge could have expressed himself in similar language. The vexed question of a profession was now finally set at rest. Unitarianism had banished

---

[1] In 1836 Southey made an effort to repudiate his share in the "vain visions." He protested that the scheme of Pantisocrasy was introduced by Coleridge and his friend Hucks.

all idea of the Church ; the dragoon regiment had imperilled the chances of college honours and a college life ;
authorship was a refuge for which none of the young men
were yet sufficiently destitute ; so colonization on a fresh
principle, akin to that of the early apostles, who had all
things in common, supplied the motive power for a great
start in life. But Pantisocrasy was something more
serious than the crutch that was to help a lame dog over
a stile. It was to be the nucleus of a great socialistic
regeneration.

The scheme was incomplete when the young men
arrived at Bristol, and there it made notable strides. It
was decided that a ship must be chartered to take the
party to the New World, that land must be purchased
either before they set out or on their arrival in America ;
that a body of farming implements must be bought and
taken with them. But, above all, it was agreed and
settled that for the future welfare of the colony, as well
as for its immediate comfort and harmony, it would be
necessary that each male colonist should be accompanied
by a wife. This final condition was not a barrier. One
of the Pantisocritans was already provided with a wife,
two were about to be so provided, and it was not anticipated that the rest would fail in this regard. The more
material conditions were a deal more troublesome.
Chartering a ship and buying implements and land were
processes involving the expenditure of money, and the
Pantisocritans were penniless. They were, however, rich
in hope, and looked confidently to a near future in which
they should be rich enough in money also to realize their
dream. At Bristol they talked over their plans, discussed

them, made proselytes, made enemies, were admired, and were laughed at. Coleridge was too much alone in the world now for any one to care what practicable future he relinquished for a vain and visionary scheme. But Southey had a rich aunt who turned her back upon him, and the Somersetshire father of Burnet was not so well content with farming as to approve of it in its newest disguise. The positions and prospects of certain of the proselytes are not ascertainable, but we know that a man-servant of Southey's angry aunt belonged to the little band. This leal fellow, Shadrack by name, had "a prime hot berth" of it after his apostasy had become known, and when one night Southey was turned out of doors in the wet, he said: "Why, sir, you be'nt goin' to Bath at this time o' night, and in this weather!" The trusty soul was rewarded with true Pantisocratic fraternity. In a very large hand, Coleridge—Logician, Metaphysician, Bard—wrote these touching words: "SHAD GOES WITH US: HE IS MY BROTHER!" One cannot resist the conclusion that in the fiery furnace of their enthusiasm, there some-times flickered a tiny jet of conscious travesty.

Coleridge returned to Cambridge to keep the Michaelmas Term. Back in his rooms at college he writes: "Since I quitted this room what and how im-portant events have been evolved! America! Southey! Miss Fricker! . . . Pantisocrasy! Oh, I shall have such a scheme of it! My head, my heart, are all alive." During the remainder of the term his head was not only alive, but as sore as that of a bear in its cage. He left Cambridge towards December, and went up to London There he met Dyer, author of "Complaints of the Poor,"

and found him an eager partizan.   Dyer was enraptured
with the system, pronounced it impregnable, and believed
that his friend, Dr. Priestley, would join the Pantisocritans.   He does not appear to have mentioned a desire
to join them himself.   One great stride was now made—
the place of settlement in the New World was decided
upon.   " Every night," wrote Coleridge, " I meet a most
intelligent young man, who has spent the last five years
of his life in America, and is lately come from thence as
an agent to sell land.   He was of our school.   I had
been kind to him ; he remembers it, and comes regularly
every evening to 'benefit by my conversation,' he says.
He says £2,000 will do ; that he doubts not we can
contract for our passage under £400 ; that we shall buy
the land a great deal cheaper when we arrive in America
than we could in England ; or 'why,' he adds, 'am I
sent over here ? '   That twelve men may *easily* clear three
hundred acres in four or five months ; and that for six
hundred dollars a thousand acres may be cleared, and
houses built on them.   He recommends the Susquehanna
from its excessive beauty and security from hostile
Indians. . . . That literary characters may make *money*
there, etc., etc.   The mosquitos there are not so bad as
our gnats, and after you have been there a little while
they don't trouble you."

It was all so beautifully clear and simple.   Two thousand pounds would do ; the Susquehanna was free from
hostile Indians, although it had so recently been desolated
by them ; literary characters could even make money
there, and the mosquitos in a little while did not bite.
The place of resort at which Coleridge met every night

the intelligent young man from America was a smoky
little room in a pot-house in Newgate Street, known
as the "Salutation and Cat." There in an odour of
tobacco, egg-hot, and welsh rabbit, Coleridge discoursed
nightly on poetry and metaphysics as well as on Pantisocrasy. The intelligent young man was not the only
person who came every evening to benefit by Coleridge's
conversation. Tradition says that when the time came
for Coleridge to go to Bristol to be married, the landlord
offered him free quarters if he would stay and talk.
Long years afterwards the same offer was made to the
poet's son, poor "laal Hartley," by the landlord of a
certain "Red Lion" far away north among the mountains.
In the smoky room of the "Salutation," Coleridge
renewed his friendship with his old schoolfellow, Charles
Lamb. Charles was now nineteen years old to Coleridge's
two and twenty. When his friend went up to the University,
Lamb had been apprenticed to the "desk's dry wood,"
and he was now a clerk in the India House. Looking
longingly towards the career of learning which he was
never to enjoy, he went on patiently writing the "books"
that were never, never to be read. His father was falling
into dotage ; his mother was sickly ; his sister was a
brave, stricken soul, fighting the battle of life at awful
odds. As needs must be, Charles plodded on in his
beaten round with the docility of a mill horse, and some
of its slumbering strength as well. But there were secret
ambitions nestling deep down in hidden places, and when
Coleridge came back to London full of glorious schemes,
the dark pillar of hope just turning its face of fire—what
a time it was for Lamb ! Amid the associations of pipes

and oronokoo, in that dear little dirty pot-house in Newgate Street, how they talked and laughed and drank!
And were ever friends more unlike—Coleridge, the
eloquent madcap of genius, the dreamer of high
dreams; Lamb with a dismal void in his heart, with
his lisp and his half-playful, half-melancholy smile! In
that smoky room Coleridge recited his newest poems in
his deep intonation, and Lamb—cheated of his grief—
applauded them in his sweet, broken accents. What
Lamb thought of Pantisocrasy is not known. Coleridge
had too deep a sense of the tragedy in the life of his
friend to tempt him from his post of duty. What a
friendship it was that really began in that odour of egg-
hot and oronokoo! In loyalty, in beauty, in love, does
the like of it appear elsewhere?

Whether Coleridge availed himself of the landlord's
offer is not stated, but it is certain that he " stayed " and
" talked." There is an idea that he stayed too long, in
the judgment of the young lady who was waiting for him
at Bristol. It is even said that the scrupulous Southey
felt constrained to point out to his friend that he had
gone too far in his attentions to Miss Fricker for any
honourable retreat. But the poet was busy with poetry.
He was printing his first sonnets in *The Morning Chronicle*,
and finishing his " Religious Musings." [1]

[1] Writing to Cottle (March 6, 1836), Southey says : " Coleridge
did not come back again to Bristol till January, 1795, nor would he,
I believe, *have come back at all*, if I had not gone to London to look
for him, for having got there from Cambridge at the beginning of
the winter, there he remained, without writing a line either to Miss
Fricker or myself." The punctilious Southey searched for Coleridge
at the smoky tavern in Newgate Street, but found him at the " Angel
Inn," Butcher Hall Street, and carried him off to be married.

It was a mistake to think that he was not ardently in love. He returned to Miss Fricker, and to Pantisocrasy, early in 1795. These two, the lady and the system, sailed in one boat. Two thousand pounds would do to make everything "perfectly delightful"; but then it began to appear that "money" was "a huge evil," which the Pantisocritans would long have to contend with. In this older hemisphere the literary characters could make anything easier than money, and the gnats of the literary world were worse than the mosquitos of Susquehanna. A publisher in London offered Coleridge six guineas for a volume of poetry. The poets lectured at Bristol with only moderate success. Things were beginning to wear a grave aspect, when one day Cottle, the Bristol bookseller, said to Coleridge, "To encourage you, I will give you thirty guineas for your poems, and to make you easy you shall have the money as your occasions require." Silence and the grasped hand showed that the poet was happy. He then lost no time in getting married; and Southey, to whom a similar offer had been made, soon followed suit. Coleridge was married Oct. 4th; and Southey Nov. 14, 1795, both at St. Mary's, Redcliffe, the church in which Chatterton, twenty-seven years before, pretended to find his Rowley forgeries. Marriage had always been regarded as a condition of harmony in the grand system, but nevertheless it introduced the first note of discord. The visionary Southey, who had sacrificed a rich aunt to Pantisocrasy, began to sober down into a person of practical mind at the near approach of his wedding-day. An uncle offered him a trip to Lisbon; he saw money in the offer, and accepted. Coleridge is described as wrath beyond words, though a reasonable, or unreasonable, supply of words appears to have been forthcoming. But Coleridge was himself married by this time, and we may suspect that his anger (if he felt any, which Southey denied) was akin to that of Hamlet when he finds his uncle praying—a colourable cover for a personal exit. Poor Robert Lovell took a fever at Salisbury, and died; and George Burnet, and the intelligent young man from America, dropped as surely out of the history. So did Pantisocrasy go to the wall; and twenty-six adventurers, who were to have regenerated society, went quietly back to the world.

CHAPTER IV.

COLERIDGE took a cottage at Clevedon, near Bristol. It was a pretty little place, one storey high, with a rose-tree peeping in at the chamber window. The parlour was whitewashed, but then the rent was only five pounds a year. A young couple who had made up their minds to a hut in the clearing of a forest, where the bison and the Red Indian were not unknown, could hardly be unhappy in a primitive little cabin on the banks of the Severn. Coleridge was fully content, and took a practical view of his environment. "Send me," he writes to Cottle, "a riddle slice, a candle-box, two glasses for the wash-hand stand, one dustpan, one small tin tea-kettle, one pair of candlesticks, a Bible, a keg of porter," etc., etc. The bookseller sent the poet everything, not forgetting the Bible, in which Coleridge duly entered the date of his marriage, leaving spaces for the entry, in due time, of the births of his children. Mrs. Coleridge was a happy young wife in these early days. Coleridge used to say that, like his mother, she had no meretricious accomplishments. She was "an honest, simple, lively-minded, affectionate woman." Pretty and agreeable, able to sing a little, and

even to write poetry that was far from contemptible, she
was a comfortable and a practical wife for a man of somewhat changeable temper. Coleridge had now drifted into
literature as a profession. His two inexorable taskmasters, bread and cheese, made no terms with any
less material deities, and even poetry had to make way
for a pursuit that should be something more than its
"own exceeding great reward." While passing his
volume of poems through the press, he was writing for
The Morning Chronicle and *The Critical Review*. His
prospects were doubtful, his earnings uncertain, and he
had many projects. Not long after settling at Clevedon
he was offered a school at Derby. About the same time
he had the chance of a Unitarian pulpit at Nottingham.
A tutorship at Bristol came his way, and Roscoe invited
him to pitch his tent in Liverpool. The editor of *The
Morning Chronicle* offered a sort of joint-editorship, and
he was tempted to remove to London. " I am forced to
write for my bread!" he says; "write the flights of
poetic enthusiasm, when every minute I am hearing a
groan from my wife! Groans and complaints and sickness! . . . The future is cloud and darkness! Poverty,
perhaps, and the thin faces of them that want bread,
looking up at me!" This was written in a passing fit
of despondency, but the general sense conveyed of uncertainty and anxiety was sufficiently abiding. Coleridge
thought he had solved the problem of livelihood necessity, when one day he conceived the idea of a weekly
journal. It was to be a newspaper, review, and annual
register combined. The title was to be *The Watchman*,
and the miscellany was to " cry the state of the political

atmosphere." It was to be published every eighth day.
Coleridge first called a meeting of friends in Bristol, to
discuss the project, and then set out on a canvassing tour
for subscribers through the Midland and Northern
counties, armed with many copies of a flaming prospectus. Surely no such canvasser ever before " took
the road ; " and the story of the canvass is probably the
most humorous narrative that ever came from Coleridge's
pen. His campaign began at Birmingham, and his first
attack was on a rigid Calvinist, a tallow-chandler by trade.
With plentiful lack of worldly wisdom, the young author,
trading on his own account, commenced an harangue of
half-an-hour, varying his notes through the whole gamut
of eloquence, from the ratiocinative to the declamatory.
He argued, he promised, he prophesied, and beginning
with the captivity of nations, he ended with the near-
approach of the millennium. The man of tallow listened
with noble patience, and then said, after a pause, " And
what, sir, might the cost be ? " " Only fourpence ! " Oh,
the bathos of that fourpence ! There was another pause,
and then the man of lights said, " That comes to a deal
of money at the end of the year. How much did you
say there would be for the money ? Thirty-two pages ?
Bless me ! Why, except what I does in a family way on
the Sabbath, that's more than I ever reads, sir, all the
year round. I am as great a one as any man in Brum-
magen, sir, for liberty and truth, and all them sort of
things, but as to this, no offence, I hope, sir, I must beg
to be excused."

So ended Coleridge's first canvass. On the opening
night of the tour he was to meet a number of political

friends and discuss the projected miscellany. After dinner, his host importuned him to smoke a pipe. The poet declined, chiefly on the ground that he had never smoked since the nights at the "Salutation," and then it had been herb tobacco, mixed with oronokoo. Assured that the tobacco in this instance was equally mild, and being of a disposition that made it hard to say no, Coleridge took half a pipe; but giddiness ensued, and the pipe was soon abandoned. Then he sallied forth to meet his friends at the house of a Birmingham minister. The walk and the fresh air intensified the unpleasant symptoms of sickness, and he had scarcely entered the minister's drawing-room, when he sank back on the sofa in a swoon. There he lay, with a face like a wall that is whitewashed, deadly pale, and with cold drops of perspiration running down from his forehead, when one by one the gentlemen dropped in who had been invited to meet and spend the evening with him. The effects of the tobacco wore off, and the poet looked round on the party, his bleared eyes blinking in the candle-light. To relieve the embarrassment, one of the patriots said, "Have you seen a paper to-day, Mr. Coleridge?" Coleridge raised himself, and rubbed his eyes. "Sir," he said, in a solemn tone, "I am far from convinced that a Christian is permitted to read either newspapers or any other works of merely political and temporal interest." The ludicrous incongruity of the remark was too much for the risibility of the Birmingham gentlemen, and there was an involuntary burst of laughter, in which, after a moment's reflection, the poet joined.

The eloquence which failed to impress the tallow-chandler inspired admiration and astonishment in more sympathetic minds, and Coleridge's canvass was a brilliant success. He returned to Bristol with about a thousand subscribers, and issued his first number of *The Watchman* on the 1st of March, 1796. He worked hard at tasks that were the reverse of congenial—condensing parliamentary reports, arranging foreign and domestic intelligence, and the like. It would not do. Dissatisfaction began to show itself among the subscribers at an early stage. One man thought he did not get enough for his fourpence; another was of opinion that his boys did not profit under the publication; a third wanted more reviews; a fourth demanded more politics; some of the subscribers gave up the paper because it did not contain sufficient original composition, and a far larger number abandoned it because it contained too much. And of all men on earth Coleridge was the most likely to be fretted by such perplexities. *The Watchman* went on to May 14th, having passed through ten numbers, and then it ceased to cry the state of the political atmosphere. "The reason for relinquishing it," said the editor, "is short and simple—the work does not pay for its expenses." Back numbers of the miscellany were more than plentiful at the house of the proprietor. One morning Coleridge found the servant girl lighting the fire with some copies. "What have you there?" he asked. "La, sir, it's only *Watchmans*," the girl answered.

In April, 1796, Coleridge's first volume of poems appeared. It attracted no special attention. *The Monthly Review* observed that though poets had been called maniacs, and their writings too frequently justified the application of the degrading epithet, yet as it was time to enthrone reason on the summit of Parnassus, Mr. Coleridge seemed solicitous to consecrate his noble lyre to truth, virtue, and humanity. Poor fustian as this may be, it seems to be all that the critical press had to put forth. Later in the year Coleridge printed privately an anthology of twenty-four sonnets; and later still he published his "Ode to the Departing Year." In 1796 Southey's "Joan of Arc" appeared, and in that poem there were about four hundred lines by Coleridge. Thus was Coleridge fairly launched as a poet.

The poet and his wife had grown weary of Clevedon; it was too far from the city library; it was difficult of access to friends, and the neighbours were tattling and inquisitive. Moreover, Mrs. Coleridge was looking forward to her first confinement. So they returned to Bristol. There is reason to think that at this period Coleridge paid another visit to his native place, and that the family unpleasantness was thereby much modified. The poet had previously made some concessions in the pathetic epistle to his brother George. With the failure of *The Watchman* the old embarrassments began to press heavily. There was always an idea that a Unitarian pulpit might be found for Coleridge. He preached twice in Bath, when he dressed for the pulpit in a blue coat and white waistcoat, and on several occasions during his canvass, when he permitted his garments of various hue to be enveloped in the sable gown. He was not an impressive preacher. His first sermon was delivered to a congregation of seventeen persons. The discourse

was on the Hair Powder Tax, and before it was half
done one of the seventeen opened his pew silently and
stole quietly out of the chapel. In a few minutes more
a second auditor did the same; then a third, and a fourth.
Matters looked ominous. It seemed as if in a short
time every pew would be empty. Still the preacher
went on without any consciousness of what was happen-
ing, and finished with great self-content. There is a
fable which says that beside Coleridge's personal friends
there was one elderly lady who sat out the sermon quite
stoically ; but then she was asleep. The pulpit was not
destined to hold Coleridge's wings ; the idea of making
the poet a Unitarian minister came to nothing. The
twin taskmasters, bread and cheese, were again inexorable, when a new friend, Thomas Poole, invited the poet
to Nether Stowey, Somersetshire, where a comfortable
cottage at seven pounds a year was to be rented near to
his own home. Poole was a prosperous tanner, a cul-
tured man who had travelled extensively. He had a
luxurious house and a good library, and was anxious to
secure Coleridge as a neighbour. The poet saw in the
proposal a chance of retrenching domestic expenses.
About the same time one of the gentlemen whom
Coleridge met in Birmingham, on the memorable occasion of his essay in smoking, suggested that his son
should lodge with the poet for the benefit of that society
which was in itself a liberal education. Both proposals
were accepted. Thus did Coleridge temporize with his
necessities. His first child, Hartley, was born in Bristol
in September, 1796, and soon afterwards the Coleridge
household, including Charles Lloyd, a young man of

literary tastes and some literary pretensions, was settled at Nether Stowey.

The twin taskmasters were temporarily appeased, and the poet wrote more at leisure than before. He had carried on a correspondence with Lamb since the nights at the "Salutation and Cat." The interval had witnessed many changes in the life of his schoolfellow. Lamb's father had fallen into dotage, and been pensioned off by his employer. His mother was now deprived of the use of her limbs. These two had been pleasure-loving people in their time, and now they were exacting invalids. The burden of their sickness and society had fallen upon Charles and his sister Mary, whose elder brother, a selfish, unamiable soul, had carried himself off to a more comfortable home. The resources of the household were limited. They had removed from their rooms in the Temple to poorer lodgings in Little Queen Street, Holborn. Charles's salary was hardly more than a hundred pounds a year, and his father's pension was not material. A querulous old aunt lived with the family, and contributed towards the general maintenance. Mary became a needlewoman, and had a young girl for apprentice. It was a straitened sort of existence, but Charles and his sister bore up under it as well as they could. Not long after Coleridge's return to Bristol, at the beginning of 1795, Lamb's reason gave way. He was six weeks in a mad-house. When he recovered his reason, his heart was a void; hope was not easily regained. He toiled on, and was stimulated by his correspondence with Coleridge. The old schoolfellows discussed poetry and religion. But there was not much time for such indul-

gences. The day was given to the " desk's dry wood,"
and the nights to cribbage with his poor crazy father.
" If you will not play with me, you might as well not
come home," said the old man one night when his son
had taken up pen and paper. " There is nothing to say
to that," Lamb thought, and so he took up the cards.
It was a paralysing situation. And Charles was not
more deeply involved than Mary. That pure soul had
no touch of selfishness. Night and day she toiled for
her helpless mother, without even the reward of gratitude. The mother was a woman of a different mould, and
the daughter's very caresses were often met by coldness
and repulsion. Still she held on until reason became
unsettled. " Polly, what are those poor crazy moythered
brains of yours thinking of always?" the grandmother
used to say. The tragedy reached a catastrophe at
length. One day, about the middle of September, 1796,.
the " poor crazy moythered brains " led Mary to snatch
up a knife and make a sudden attack upon her apprentice.
The girl escaped, but the invalid mother interposed, and
Mary's frenzy was then directed towards her. Charles
was near, but he was only in time to snatch the knife out
of his sister's hand when its dreadful work was done.
Mary had killed her mother. Her father had also been
wounded in the forehead. Mary was removed. That
night while the body of the mother lay in their little
lodging, the old aunt lay insensible, like one dying.
Charles was very calm, though brought down to the
depths of nervous misery. He dared not give way, for he
had his own reason to hold in command. An inquest
brought in a verdict of insanity, and Mary was removed

to the asylum at Islington. While the coroner was sitting, Charles was required to play cards with his father. On the second day after the day of horrors some twenty people came to the lodgings to talk and eat and " make merry." Then the tension could be borne no longer. In an agony of indignation, rage, and something like remorse, Charles found his way mechanically to the room where his dead mother lay, and fell on his knees by the side of her coffin. Alone in his awful misery he poured out his heart in letters to Coleridge, his only friend, and Coleridge answered him in these noble words :—

"Your letter, my friend, struck me with a mighty horror. It rushed upon me and stupefied my feelings. You bid me write you a religious letter. I am not a man who would attempt to insult the greatness of your anguish by any other consolation. Heaven knows that in the easiest fortunes there is much dissatisfaction and weariness of spirit ; much that calls for the exercise of patience and resignation ; but in storms like these that shake the dwelling and make the heart tremble, there is no middle way between despair and the yielding up of the whole spirit to the guidance of faith. And surely it is a matter of joy that your faith in Jesus has been preserved ; the Comforter that should relieve you is not far from you. But as you are a Christian, in the name of that Saviour who was filled with bitterness and made drunken with wormwood, I conjure you to have recourse in frequent prayer to ' His God and your God,' the God of mercies and Father of all comfort. Your poor father is, I hope, almost senseless to the calamity ; the unconscious instrument of Divine Providence knows it not; and your mother is in Heaven. It is sweet to be roused from a frightful dream by the song of birds, and the gladsome rays of the morning. Ah, how infinitely more sweet to be awakened from the blackness and amazement of a sudden horror by the glories of God manifest, and the hallelujahs of angels.

"As to what regards yourself, I approve altogether of your abandoning what you justly call vanities. I look upon you as a man called by sorrow and anguish, and a strange desolation of hopes, into quietness, and a soul set apart and made peculiar to God; we cannot arrive at any portion of heavenly bliss without, in some measure, imitating Christ. And they arrive at the largest inheritance who imitate the most difficult parts of His character, and, bowed down and crushed under foot, cry, in fulness of faith, 'Father, Thy will be done.'

"I wish above measure to have you for a little while here; no visitants shall blow on the nakedness of your feelings; you shall be quiet, that your spirit may be healed. I see no possible objection, unless your father's helplessness prevent you, and unless you are necessary to him. If this be not the case, I charge you write me that you will come.

"I charge you, my dearest friend, not to dare to encourage gloom or despair; you are a temporary sharer in human miseries, that you may be an eternal partaker of the Divine nature. I charge you, if by any means it be possible, come to me."

Lamb rose above his great sorrow. In the first hours of his trial he had tried to cut himself away from every pursuit that was not directly sanctified by religion. "Mention nothing of poetry," he wrote. "I have destroyed every vestige of past vanities of that kind. . . . I charge you, don't think of coming to see me. Write. I will not see you if you come. God Almighty love you and all of us." He begged Coleridge to be reconciled to his family. For his own part he intended to put by all thought of love and marriage, and give up his life, while reason and strength remained to him, to the afflicted of his desolated household. But stage by stage he returned to the things of the world. Mary came back to reason and to a quiet and touching consciousness of what had happened, and death took their father from his imbecility. Then the sun began to shine with a subdued radiance on the lives of brother and sister. Charles wrote poetry as before, and when a second edition of Coleridge's poems appeared in 1797 the little volume included poems both by Lamb and Lloyd. Let us reflect on the ennobling effects of noble pain, and we may be pardoned for wondering that after passing through this furnace of affliction Charles Lamb did not grow to a yet loftier stature of manhood. The marvel is not so much that he was great, as that he was not greater.

CHAPTER V.

A T Stowey, affairs went on satisfactorily. "We are all—wife, bantling, and self, remarkably well." Coleridge wrote : " Mrs. Coleridge loves Stowey, and loves Thomas Poole and his mother, who love her. . . . Our house is better than we expected—there is a comfortable bedroom and sitting-room for C. Lloyd, and another for us, a room for Nanny, a kitchen and out-house. . . . We have a pretty garden, . . . and I am already an expert gardener, and both my hands can exhibit a callum as testimonials of their industry. . . . A communication has been made from our orchard into T. Poole's garden, and from thence to Cruikshank's, a friend of mine, and a young married man, whose wife is very amiable, . . . and from all this you will conclude we are happy." Succeeding letters give hint of a less favourable condition. It turned out that Charles Lloyd was subject to fits, and the domestic quiet of Coleridge's home was thereby seriously disturbed. Immediately before the removal from Bristol, Coleridge met for the first time William Wordsworth, the author of " Descriptive Sketches," the book which in his judgment had signalized the advent of a great poetic genius. Wordsworth, the son of an attorney, was born

in Cockermouth, Cumberland, about two years before
Coleridge's birth in Devonshire.　At seventeen he went
up to Cambridge, and in 1791, when Coleridge was
preparing to enter the University, Wordsworth was
preparing to leave it.　They had not met at Cambridge,
and Coleridge's first knowledge of Wordsworth was
gathered from the poems published in 1793.　Wordsworth
went from Cambridge to London, stayed there some
time, and then visited North Wales on a pedestrian tour
with a friend.　Coleridge took the same course three
years later.　In the autumn of 1791, Wordsworth went
to Paris, and from thence to Orleans and Blois, remaining abroad some thirteen months.　Between the beginning
of 1793, when Coleridge was being enmeshed in the debts
which led to his career as a dragoon, and the beginning of
1796, Wordsworth lived among friends in London and elsewhere.　He had been counselled to take orders, and was
offered a curacy at Harwich, but his sympathies were, at
least temporarily, estranged from the Church.　He tried
to establish a newspaper.　The scheme came to nothing,
and a good deal of political enthusiasm on the side of
the democracy found no immediate outlet.　A friend
named Calvert, left him a legacy of £900, and on the
interest of this sum he contrived to live.　His volume
of poetry had no special success.　*The Monthly Review*
(1793), a recognized authority, reviewed the book in
these terms : " More descriptive poetry !　Have we not
yet enough ?　Must eternal changes be rung on upland
and lowland, and nodding forests, and brooding clouds,
and cells, and dells, and dingles ?　Yes ; more and yet
more : so it is decreed."　The critic quoted the familiar

simile about the purple morning falling over the mountain-
side in flakes of light, and expressed sorrow at seeing the
purple morning confined so like a maniac in a strait-
waistcoat. Such was Wordsworth's reception. In 1797,
he held no position as a poet. Before this time Coleridge
was beginning to be talked about. Wordsworth had
heard of him, and he went over to Bristol to see him.
He was then settled with his sister, Dorothy Wordsworth,
a woman of education and refined feeling, at Racedown
in Dorsetshire. Rather later Coleridge visited Words
worth, and was much stimulated by his conversation.
They had a good deal in common. Their political
sympathies were akin, and their poetic taste was similiar.
Both were at work on tragedies, Coleridge's tragedy
" Osorio," having been begun in the hope—not without
grounds of assurance—that Sheridan would consider it
for Drury Lane. Wordsworth's tragedy, "The Borderers,"
was to be introduced to the manager of Covent Garden.
" I am sojourning for a few days at Racedown, Dorset,
the mansion of our friend Wordsworth ; who presents his
kindest regards to you," writes Coleridge to Cottle.
"Wordsworth admires my tragedy, which gives me great
hopes. Wordsworth has written a tragedy himself. I
speak with heart-felt sincerity, and, I think, unblinded
judgment, when I tell you that I feel myself a little man
by his side, and yet I do not think myself a less man
than I formerly thought myself. His drama is absolutely
wonderful." At a later date Coleridge writes with yet
more emphasis : " The giant Wordsworth—God love
him ! When I speak in the terms of admiration due to
his intellect, I fear lest these terms should keep out of

sight the amiableness of his manners. He has written near twelve hundred lines of blank verse, superior, I hesitate not to aver, to anything in our language which any way resembles it." Wordsworth's impressions of Coleridge can hardly have been less favourable than language like this implies. When Coleridge removed to Stowey, Wordsworth removed to Alfoxden, to be near enough to enjoy Coleridge's society. It is from Dorothy Wordsworth that we get the record of the early days of the friendship now begun. " Coleridge is a wonderful man," she writes, "his face teems with mind, soul, and spirit. Then he is so benevolent, so good-tempered and cheerful. . . . At first I thought him plain—that is, for about three minutes : he is pale, thin, has a wide mouth, thick lips, and not very good teeth, longish, loose-growing, half-curling, rough black hair. . . . His eye is large and full, and not very dark, but grey, such an eye as would receive from a heavy soul the dullest expression ; but it speaks every emotion of his animated mind : it has more of 'the poet's eye in a fine frenzy rolling,' than I have ever witnessed. He has fine dark eyebrows, and over-hanging forehead." Of Wordsworth's sister, Coleridge has left an equally graphic picture. " She is a woman indeed ! " he said, " in mind, I mean, and heart ; for her person is such, that if you expected to see a pretty woman you would think her rather ordinary ; if you expected to see an ordinary woman you would think her pretty ! " There is a suspicion that Coleridge's wife was not altogether so well pleased with her new neighbours. Miss Words-worth is said to have angered Mrs. Coleridge by making free with her shawls, and by taking long walks with her husband.   Such were the beginnings of one of the most memorable of literary friendships.   It resulted in a poetic movement of the highest importance in the history of English letters ; and it was beautiful, and pathetic, and lasting in itself.   No doubt each of these vigorous and original minds influenced the other ; but it would be vain to try to estimate the reciprocation of influence.

The friends met often, and their conversation turned contantly on two cardinal points of poetry, " the power of exciting the sympathy of the reader by a faithful adherence to the truth of nature, and the power of giving the interest of novelty by the modifying colours of the imagination." They thought of the sudden charm which moonlight or sunset gives to a familiar landscape, and this combination of the actual and familiar with the glamour of the supernatural appeared to say that the two cardinal points of poetry—reality and imagination—might be united. The thought then suggested itself, that on this basis a series of poems could be composed of two sorts.   In the one the incidents and agents were to be in part supernatural ; in the other, the characters and incidents were to be chosen from ordinary village life.   Coleridge was to direct himself to the romantic element, and to give to supernatural incidents the reality of human interest. Wordsworth, on the other hand, was to propose to himself a series of realistic themes, and to give a charm analogous to that of the supernatural to things of everyday life.   The result of this idea was the poems known as the " Lyrical Ballads."   Coleridge wrote for his share " The Rime of the Ancient Mariner," " The Dark Ladie," and the first part of " Christabel."   Wordsworth wrote a much larger body of poetry in pursuance of the scheme.

This account of the origin of the "Lyrical Ballads" is practically Coleridge's. But Wordsworth's statement, though not irreconcilable with that of his brother poet, is distinctly more prosaic. Wordsworth says that in the autumn of 1797 he started from Alfoxden with his sister and Coleridge, with a view to visit Linton and the Valley of Rocks. The united funds were very small, and they agreed to defray the expenses of the tour by writing a poem to be sent to *The Monthly Magazine.* Accordingly, in the course of their walk, they planned the poem of the "Ancient Mariner," founded on a dream of a friend of Coleridge, the Mr. Cruikshank who was his neighbour at Stowey. Much the greater part of the story was Coleridge's invention, but certain parts Wordsworth suggested. "For example," says Wordsworth, "some crime to be committed which would bring upon the Old Navigator, as Coleridge afterwards delighted to call him, the spectral persecution, as a consequence of that crime and his own wanderings. I had been reading in Shelvocke's 'Voyages,' a day or two before, that, while doubling Cape Horn, they frequently saw albatrosses in that latitude, the largest sort of sea-fowl, some extending their wings twelve or thirteen feet. 'Suppose,' said I, 'you represent him as having killed one of these birds on entering the South Sea, and that the tutelary spirits of these regions take upon them to avenge the crime?' The incident was thought fit for the purpose, and adopted accordingly." The poets began the composition together on that evening, but their respective manners proved so widely different, that Wordsworth withdrew from the undertaking. In Coleridge's hands the poem grew until it became too important for their first object, which was limited to the earning of five pounds, and they began to think of a volume which was to consist of poems chiefly on supernatural subjects.

It is certain that Coleridge's poetic genius was much stimulated by Wordsworth's conversation. Besides writing the " Ancient Mariner," " The Dark Ladie," and the first part of " Christabel "—poems that were intended to realize the preconceived ideal—Coleridge finished his tragedy " Osorio," and wrote " The Three Graves," " Fears in Solitude," " France, an Ode," and " Kubla Khan,"[1] during the period in which he and Wordsworth

[1] The circumstances attending the composition of " Kubla Khan " are sufficiently curious to merit a separate statement. This is Coleridge's account : " In the summer of the year 1797, the author, then in ill health, had retired to a lonely farmhouse between Porlock and Lynton, on the Exmoor confines of Somerset and Devonshire. In consequence of a slight indisposition, an anodyne had been prescribed, from the effect of which he fell asleep in his chair at the moment that he was reading the following sentence, or words of the same substance, in ' Purchas's Pilgrimage ' : ' Here the Khan Kubla commanded a palace to be built, and a stately garden thereunto : and thus ten miles of fertile ground were inclosed with a wall.' The author continued for about three hours in a profound sleep, at least of the external senses, during which time he has the most vivid confidence, that he could not have composed less than from two to three hundred lines ; if that indeed can be called composition in which all the images rose up before him as things, with a parallel production of the correspondent expressions, without any sensation or consciousness of effort. On awaking he appeared to himself to have a distinct recollection of the whole, and taking his pen, ink, and paper, instantly and eagerly wrote down the lines that

were near neighbours. That period was probably the happiest in his life. Free from pecuniary embarrassments, Coleridge was no longer singing like the nightingale with his breast against a thorn. His earnings must have been inconsiderable. He was probably writing for *The Morning Chronicle*, *The Critical Review*, and occasionally for *The Monthly Magazine*. His expenses were small, and Charles Lloyd was there to share them. That domestic partnership must have had its humiliating side ; it certainly had its vexatious accompaniment ; but Coleridge does not seem to have complained. With small earnings and small necessities, and the work and the society he loved, he appears to have lived a life of more thorough content than had fallen to his lot before. Charles Lamb and his sister visited him at Stowey, and made the acquaintance of Lloyd. Cottle was with him also. Wordsworth, his sister, Coleridge, and Cottle made one memorable excursion of pleasure. The party set out from Bristol in a gig, well laden with philosophers' viands, a bottle of brandy, a loaf, a piece of cheese, and a bunch of lettuces. On the road they gave something to a beggar, and the sturdy ingrate is suspected of having extracted their cheese while they were gazing at the clouds. They realized their loss at the moment when

are here preserved. At this moment he was unfortunately called out by a person on business from Porlock, and detained by him above an hour, and on his return to his room, found, to his no small surprise and mortification, that though he still retained some vague and dim recollection of the general purport of the vision, yet with the exception of some eight or ten scattered lines and images, all the rest had passed away like the images on the surface of a stream into which a stone had been cast."

they drove into the courtyard of the house wherein they intended to dine ; and there a more unwonted adventure awaited them. The horse was taken out of the gig and led to the stable. Obviously the harness had to be taken off, but to remove the collar proved to be a perplexing difficulty. Cottle and Wordsworth attempted the task, and both relinquished it as impracticable. Then Coleridge, the ex-dragoon, tried his hand, and soon showed such grooming skill that he almost twisted the horse's neck to strangulation, affirming that it must have grown by dropsy or gout since the collar was put on. At their utmost point of despair, a servant girl came up and said, " La, master, you do not go about the work in the right way ; you should do like this," and then she turned the collar upside down, and slipped it off in a moment.

Wordsworth and Coleridge made many excursions over the Quantock Hills. Their occupations being unknown to the peasantry, the rumour became current that they were conspirators meditating an outrage. This blunder went so far that a spy was sent down to watch their movements. One night the fellow got drunk at the inn, and told his errand and history.

In 1798 Cottle published at Bristol the first volume of the " Lyrical Ballads," containing, as Coleridge's contribution, " The Rime of the Ancient Mariner," " The Foster Mother's Tale," " The Nightingale," and " The Dungeon." The book was put forth anonymously, and produced no special impression. It was alluded to in *The Monthly Review*, and in *The Critical Review* —in the latter by Southey in all probability—but the chief organs of critical opinion ignored it. The publisher lost by the transaction, and when in the course of the year he disposed of his business to Longmans, of London, he set down the copyright of the joint book at *nil*. If the poets had been supported by the hope of pecuniary benefit they were of course disappointed. To Coleridge the earnings of a successful book would have been a very material thing. His old embarrassments were beginning to reappear. Charles Lloyd had left his house. The rupture between Lloyd and Coleridge seems to have arisen out of three playful sonnets satirical of the poems of Lloyd, Lamb, and Coleridge, which had appeared in an early number of *The Monthly Magazine*. The sonnets published pseudonymously were written by Coleridge, and they were undoubtedly intended to ridicule the peculiarities of the three authors who contributed to the "Poems" published in 1797. To satirize himself anonymously was one of Coleridge's best pleasures. He did it again and again. But on this occasion he included two of his friends in his satire, and the result was a breach of friendship. Lloyd took early occasion to leave Coleridge's house, and Lamb, professing to have another cause of anger, addressed to Coleridge a most bitter letter of masked good-will on general topics, not directly dealing with their private relations. The separation from Lloyd must have led to material difficulties. Lamb's letter was, in truth, no less than an atrocious outrage inflicted in punishment of such a playful offence. Coleridge was greatly hurt, and handed the letter to Cottle, saying, "These young visionaries will do each other no good." Just at that time Lamb went on a visit to Lloyd at his father's home, and we are told that he had never appeared more cheerful. This was the only estrangement that ever divided Coleridge and Lamb. Probably it did not last long. No doubt both suffered from it. In one notable place Lamb touches with the bitterness of remorse on the freak of passion that had imperilled the love of a lifetime ; and it may be gathered that Coleridge's self-reproach was no less hard to bear. We know that the first part of " Christabel " was written in 1797. Is it possible that the noble passage on divided friends, which occurs in the second part of that poem, was written about 1798, and had a separate existence ? The joining up of the allusion to Sir Leoline and Roland is certainly clumsy, and suggests interpolation. Is it not probable that the passage had a personal significance, and that Lamb guessed its bearing ? We know that when the wise critics were unanimous in the opinion that " Christabel " was the " best nonsense-poetry ever written," Lamb was wont to say that the passage in question was enough to redeem it. In later years Lamb attributed the temporary estrangement to Lloyd's tattling. " He (Lloyd) is a sad tattler," he writes to Coleridge in 1820, " but this is under the rose. Twenty years ago he estranged one friend from me quite, whom I have been regretting, but never could regain since. He almost alienated you also from me, or me from you, I don't know which ; but that breach is closed. The ' dreary sea ' is filled up."

CHAPTER VI.

COLERIDGE'S material condition had never been worse than it was in the summer of 1798. He was twenty-seven years of age, and had now two children. In his first winter at Bristol his prospects had been brighter. He had tried many experiments towards a livelihood, and all had ended in failure. Lectures, poems, *The Watchman*, the critical reviews,—the result of every attempt had been the same. He was nothing loth to engage in very small literary enterprises, pocketing meantime his pride as a writer. His friend Cottle was no longer in business as a bookseller, and his reputation was not large enough to interest publishers with whom he had no bond of friendship. The tragedy on which he had built some hope of substantial gains had been ignored by Sheridan, and rejected by the manager at Covent Garden. Charles Lloyd had ceased to contribute to the expenses of the household, having set up his childish vanity against the abstract advantages of Coleridge's conversation as a philosopher, and the material advantages of his company as a nurse. Small debts, more humbling than larger embarrassments, debts to his shoemaker, his grocer, to his motheri-n-law, and even to his servant girl, were constantly arising to vex him. He had no fixed sources of income, or none that represented greater earnings than a guinea a week. Never was a man of great mental activity and adequate physical energy, a man with a larger capacity, and a keener anxiety for work, more hopelessly adrift in casual and unremunerative enterprises. Yet he had never lost a chance. He had never really had a chance. If in the early days of his career at Bristol some practical person had offered him a clerkship at a hundred a year, and he had rejected it, there would be more reason than there is to suspect Coleridge of deficiency in worldly wisdom. The earnings from the poems were a calculable quantity, and — Cottle's story notwithstanding — we have Coleridge's authority for saying that only fifteen of the thirty pounds were received. An offer made by the bookseller of a guinea and a half for every additional hundred lines of verse was an indefinite commission such as rarely stimulates the energy of a man who writes for his bread. It is doubtful if Coleridge ever availed himself of it. The lectures at Bristol were not highly remunerative, and the only accusation against Coleridge's practical spirit in that regard is that, for reasons not given, he broke *one* of his engagements. That the subscribers withdrew from *The Watchman* in such numbers as to make the journal an unprofitable speculation may be a charge against Coleridge's ability as a journalist, but it is certainly not an impeachment of his common sense. And if he engaged in the composition of a tragedy without sufficient knowledge of the mechanism of the stage, he did not do so without the advice and encouragement of one whose practical knowledge was beyond question. In short, the fact is clear that down to the autumn of 1798, Coleridge struggled on bravely at enormous odds, exhibiting throughout a sufficient equipment for life's battle. If moral weakness showed itself at a later period, the cause of the degeneration also became apparent. Meantime let it be said, with whatever emphasis the plain facts may justify, that vain and visionary as the youthful system called Pantisocrasy may appear, and much as we are wont to glance down at it with something of Malvolio's "demure travel of regard," the idea of betaking himself to America to farm the untouched prairie was as reasonable and practical a scheme as any other in which for four years afterwards Coleridge was permitted to engage. Pantisocrasy was not a whit less feasible, honourable, dignified, or hopeful than lecturing on French politics, and condensing English parliamentary reports, scribbling occasional verses, and talking philosophy and poetry for the benefit of the well-to-do young Birmingham gentleman of literary tastes, who paid for the poet's conversation, plus the use of his parlour and best bedroom.

Vexed by debts, and harassed by other troubles, Coleridge's mind seems to have reverted to the pulpit as a means of livelihood. A Unitarian chapel at Shrewsbury made him an offer, and he went down to that town early in 1798, to fulfil the ministerial duties. There he met a youth, William Hazlitt, who was to play an important part in his career as a public man. Hazlitt's father was a Dissenting Minister about ten miles from Shrewsbury, and he had himself been brought up with a view to the ministry, but had already abandoned that

profession in favour of art. Coleridge lodged with the
Hazlitts during his stay in Shrewsbury, and Hazlitt
has left a vivid portrait of the poet as he appeared
at this time. " His complexion," he says, " was at that
time clear and even bright. . . . His forehead was broad
and high, light as if built of ivory, with large projecting
eyebrows, and his eyes rolled beneath them like a sea
with darkening lustre. . . . His mouth was gross, volup-
tuous, open, eloquent ; his chin good-humoured and
round ; but his nose, the rudder of the face, the index of
the will, was small, feeble, nothing—like what he has
done. . . . Coleridge in his person was rather above the
common size, inclining to be corpulent. . . . His hair
(now, alas ! grey) was then black and glossy as the
raven's, and fell in smooth masses over his forehead."
More interesting still is Hazlitt's account of Coleridge's
extraordinary powers of extempore speech in the pulpit.
The effect produced by the poet on the young art
aspirant was that of a man whose insight amounted to
inspiration, whose gifts were the summit of genius.

Coleridge did not retain the Shrewsbury pulpit. From
that fresh form of intellectual slavery he was saved by
the brotherly liberality of the brothers Wedgewood.
Two of this notable family of potters, Thomas and Josiah,
sons of the first Josiah, who originated the art of English
pottery, had become friends of Coleridge in the time of
The Watchman. They were rich men, and they were
honestly interested both in their friend and in his pursuits.
Regarding with dismay the probability that the duties of
the pulpit might endanger the development of Coleridge's
genius as a poet, they made him the offer of a pension of

£150 a year (£75 to come from each), on condition that
he would devote himself to the work for which nature
had given him his best equipment.   The offer reached
the poet while he was staying with the Hazlitts, and
Hazlitt tells us that he seemed to make up his mind to
close with the proposal in the act of tying on one of his
shoes.   To learn the German language as a step towards
the practical work of translation had been for some time
a plan that Coleridge had cherished, and the Wedgewoods appear to have added to the pension the tender
of the expenses that would be incurred in a tour into
Germany.

Coleridge came to a decision with reasonable prompti-
tude.   He abandoned both the Unitarian pulpit and the
Unitarian belief.   Settling his pension on his wife and
family, he set out from Stowey for Germany in the company of Wordsworth and his sister, whose expenses were
probably defrayed by the friends who had provided for his
own.   This was in September, 1798.   The party sailed
to Hamburgh.   There the poets visited Klopstock—
Klubstick as Coleridge nicknamed him—who was then
an old man.   The friends then separated.   Wordsworth
and his sister spent a bitter winter at Goslar.   Coleridge
went on to Ratzeburg, and established himself *en pension*
with the parson.   "You have two things against you,"
Coleridge wrote to Wordsworth after they had parted :
"your not loving smoke, and your sister. If the manners of
Goslar resemble those of Ratzeburg, it is almost necessary
to be able to bear smoke.   Can Dorothy endure smoke ?
Here, when my friends come to see me, the candle nearly
goes out, the air is so thick."   From this it would appear

that Coleridge's memorable experiences at the house of
the Birmingham patriot were not without their good
effects, that he was already under weigh as a student of
the language, and that the brilliant volubility which had
distinguished him in England was producing its familiar
effects in Germany also. He spent four months at Ratzeburg, and went on to Göttingen, where, during a five
months' residence, he attended lectures on physiology and
natural history. Then he made a tour into the Hartz
Mountains in the company of three or four men whose
names became somewhat famous. His companions
describe him as ill-dressed and slovenly. He was the soul
of the party. Rhyming and poetizing, singing and punning,
and discoursing in eloquent monologue, as was his wont,
on every subject, from the captivity of nations to the near
approach of the millennium. He wrote home a series of
letters on his German tour, and they were published
many years later. These letters, entitled " Satyrane's
Letters," exhibit Coleridge's powers in a new direction.
Brilliant in style, full of suggestion, showing rare powers
of observation, keen sense of character, and a fine, racy
humour, they prove conclusively that Coleridge was not
dependent on his much-abused metaphysics for whatever
distinction he achieved as a prose writer. He remained
abroad rather less than a year, and had then acquired a
mastery of the German language. In June, 1799, he
bade farewell to Germany, and received a farewell supper
at the house of Professor Blumenbach, at Göttingen.
His health was proposed—of course amid thick air—and
he replied to the toast in fluent German, but with an
execrable accent. He arrived in England sometime in

July, proceeded at once to Stowey, and remained at home
with his wife and children until the end of August.   Then
he made a tour into Westmoreland with Wordsworth,
who was beginning to think of settling there; and in
November he came up to London, took lodgings in
Buckingham Street, Strand, and set himself to translate
Schiller's "Wallenstein" from a manuscript which had
been lent him.   In the short space of six weeks the translation was complete.   "It is a specimen of my happiest
attempt," says Coleridge, " during the prime manhood of
my intellect, before I had been buffeted by adversity or
crossed by fatality."   The translation is unquestionably a
noble production—perhaps the finest example extant of
poetry translated into poetry.   It is an amusing fact that
one of the best passages in the translation had no counter-
part in the original.   Under the impulse of strong feeling
the translator had interpolated the passage where the
poet's ardour seemed to wane, and so strongly did Schiller
feel its beauty and its fitness, that when he came to print
his trilogy in Germany, he translated Coleridge's passage
into German.   Neither poet nor translator made any note
of the liberties taken with each other.   Longmans published Coleridge's "Wallenstein" in 1800, but the book
fell quite dead in the market.   Schiller had no vogue in
England then, and Coleridge was only beginning to be
known.

The guinea a week which represented Coleridge's only
reliable income in the summer of 1798 came from Daniel
Stuart, proprietor of *The Morning Post*, with whom he
had agreed to supply occasional verses for that small
fixed sum.   The poetry which Coleridge published in

The Morning Chronicle in the days of the "Salutation and Cat," had attracted attention, and even more success of its kind attached to the poetry printed in *The Watchman.* These were days when serious literature was a factor to be counted with in the columns of a daily newspaper, and when occasional poetry had a vocation which even the leaders of public opinion could not ignore. Long afterwards Stuart tried to pass it off that he took Coleridge at the request of Mackintosh out of charity, merely to keep him from starvation. This statement is of a piece with certain other statements from the same dubious quarter. Coleridge contributed anonymously to *The Morning Post* a number of light pieces and some serious efforts, and certain of them created nothing short of a *furore.* Before going to Germany he had printed his "Fire, Famine, and Slaughter." After returning home he resumed his journalistic poetizing, and printed "The Devil's Walk." The former piece provoked a good deal of hostile feeling. It represented the deities of the title meeting in conference to describe their triumphs, and answering to the question of who unchained them, with a mysterious allusion to the name of Pitt. Its sentiment was said by some critics to be no less than diabolical. The question, "Could the writer have been other than a devil?" was discussed at a London dinner-table in the presence of the author.

Coleridge's connection with *The Morning Post* soon became a matter of consequence. Towards the end of 1799 he undertook the literary and political departments of the paper, had Wordsworth, Lamb, and Southey among his contributors, and effected such changes in its policy and in its popularity, that in a short time it more than doubled its circulation. Such at least was his own, if not Stuart's, account. Here at last was his first real chance in life. How did he deal with it? He developed into a journalist of extraordinary fecundity and resource. Stuart tried to prove the contrary, but the clear facts were all against him. Coleridge had, in a remarkable degree, the assimilative faculty which every successful journalist must possess. He wrote on a great variety of subjects with infinite allusiveness, as well as thoroughness of research. There is no reason to think that he exaggerated the effects of his labours. We have the material evidence of his employer's satisfaction. In March, 1800, after Coleridge had been four months at work, Stuart, according to Coleridge's account, offered him half-shares in his two papers, the *Post* and the *Courier*. In a letter to Poole of Stowey, Coleridge says, that if he had the least love of money he "could make sure of £2,000 a year," if he would devote himself to the two papers in conjunction with the proprietor. But Coleridge's heart was already set on a different kind of life. "I told him," he says, "that I could not give up the country and the lazy reading of old folios for two thousand times two thousand pounds—in short, that beyond £350 a year, I considered money as a real evil." In the summer of 1800 Coleridge quitted London and went up to the Lake Country. Wordsworth was already settled there, having rented and furnished a tiny cottage at Town End, Grasmere. Coleridge took half of Greta Hall, near Keswick, at twenty-five pounds a year. Like the Ancient Mariner, the old folios had their will.

Coleridge continued for two years more to write for *The Morning Post*, but his one great chance of material advantage had been permitted to go by without producing the temptation of a moment. It is easy to see that such an offer might have changed the whole current of his life. He might have become a man of substance as we say, but he deliberately elected to run his risk of being "buffeted by adversity." Does this show a deficiency in worldly wisdom? It is not for us to say so, who know what Coleridge's powers were, how much they might have put forth under favourable conditions, and how surely they must have been paralysed by the daily demands of journalism. If in the sequel those powers disappointed his own hopes, his judgment at this juncture is not chargeable with a fatality which he could not foresee. Literature has lost little by the circumstance that Coleridge did not continue to write leaders to the day of his death. The only serious loss was the material one, and that was his own, and, if any one shall say that it was his children's loss also, the answer must be that in denying himself £2,000 a year by leaving London for Keswick, Coleridge did not cut off the possibility of the £350 a year, beyond which all money was considered an evil.

CHAPTER VII.

GRETA HALL stands on the banks of the beautiful
Greta, over against Latrigg, a hill at the foot of
Skiddaw. In 1800 it was divided into two tenements,
separated by a wall. Coleridge occupied one tenement,
and the owner, Mr. Jackson, a waggoner, occupied the
other. The house is on a site which for picturesqueness
has few equals in England. Below lies a valley about
as large as the basin of Windermere. In this valley
there are two lakes, Derwentwater to the south, Bas-
senthwaite to the north, connected by a winding
river, the Derwent. Between these sheets of water,
the little town of Keswick stands. From Greta Hall
the range of view is infinite in its variety of colour and
form. To the right, you look past Castle Head and
Lodore to the mouth of Borrowdale, with Scaw Fell over
the tops of many peaks. In front, you look into
Newlands; beyond Cat Bells to the Eel Crags and
Hindsgarth. Behind you is Skiddaw with its great
chasms and bald crown. "A fairer scene," said Coleridge, "you have not seen in all your wanderings." It
was natural that the poet's romantic work should grow
amid such surroundings. Soon after settling there in

1800 he wrote the second part of " Christabel." There is little or no attempt at what is called local colour in this poem, but some Lake-country-place names are introduced.

" Christabel " was never finished. In later years Coleridge was wont to say that if a genial recurrence of the ray divine should occur for a few weeks he would attempt the completion of the poem. " If I should finish " Christabel," he said on one occasion, " I shall certainly extend it and give new characters, and a greater number. . . . I had the whole of the two cantos in my mind before I began it ; certainly the first canto is more perfect, has more of the true wild weird spirit than the last." Wordsworth had no idea how the poem was to finish, and did not think that the author had ever conceived a definite plan. Coleridge's first biographer, however, supplies from the poet's conversation a sketch of the proposed conclusion. The incidents are few as far as the poem goes. Christabel is surprised in a wood by a supernatural being, who personates the daughter, Geraldine, of an estranged friend of her father, Sir Leoline. This being tells Sir Leoline a tale of outrage and abandonment, and he determines to restore her to his old friend her father. He is about to despatch his Bard Bracy with good tidings and a message of reconciliation to Lord Roland de Vaux, when his own daughter, Christabel, betrays a strange and inexplicable repugnance to the being known as Geraldine, and prays that she may be sent away. With this posture of affairs the fragment ends. " The following relation was," says Mr. Gillman, " to have occupied a third and fourth canto, and to have

closed the tale. Over the mountains, the Bard, as
directed by Sir Leoline, hastes with his disciple ; but in
consequence of one of those inundations supposed to be
common to this country, the spot only where the castle once
stood is discovered—the edifice itself being washed away.
He determines to return. Geraldine being acquainted
with all that is passing, like the weird sisters in Macbeth,
vanishes. Re-appearing, however, she awaits the return
of the Bard, exciting in the meantime, by her wily arts,
all the anger she could rouse in the Baron's breast, as
well as that jealousy of which he is described to have
been susceptible. The old Bard and the youth at length
arrive, and therefore she can no longer personate the
character of Geraldine, the daughter of Lord Roland de
Vaux, but changes her appearance to that of the accepted
though absent lover of Christabel. Now ensues a court-
ship most distressing to Christabel, who feels, she knows
not why, great disgust for her once favoured knight. This
coldness is very painful to the Baron, who has no more
conception than herself of the supernatural transformation.
She at last yields to her father's entreaties, and consents
to approach the altar with this hated suitor. The real
lover returning, enters at this moment, and produces the
ring which she had once given him in sign of her betroth-
ment. Thus defeated, the supernatural being, Geraldine,
disappears. As predicted, the castle bell tolls, the
mother's voice is heard, and to the exceeding great joy
of the parties, the rightful marriage takes place, after
which follows a reconciliation and explanation between
the father and daughter."

Grasmere is twelve miles from Keswick, and though

the highroad is now good, the journey must have been toilsome at the beginning of the century. No doubt the customary path was the pack-horse road inside Golden Howe, and along the western bank of Thirlmere, to Wythburn, and across the Dunmail Raise. Hence with Coleridge at Greta Hall, and Wordsworth at Town End, Grasmere, it is not likely that the poets met very frequently. With fair health, and sufficient work and adequate remuneration, Coleridge appears to have passed two years at Keswick with content. "I am at present in better health than I have been," he writes, "though by no means strong and well—*and at home all is Peace and Love.*" It would not appear that he concerned himself with the dales-people about him. The strength and ruggedness of these northern folk made no impression upon his work. He on his part made no impression upon them. Not a story of Coleridge the elder seems to survive among the many traditions that gather about Greta Hall. But Coleridge learned the legends of Cumberland, and used some of them with great effect. The only instance of his interest in local affairs is that of his exertions in the case of Hatfield, the forger, who betrayed the well-known " Beauty of Buttermere." Coleridge helped to expose the scoundrel.

He continued to write for *The Morning Post*, and at the same time wrote some poetry. He kept up a correspondence with Lamb. That old friend was rising above his early sorrow, and treading down at the same time some of his early weaknesses. "My sentiment is long since vanished. I hope my virtues have done sucking," he writes. But the one was not so well banished, or the

other so well weaned, as to prevent an occasional out-
burst of agony at a return of the old pain. " I almost
wish Mary were dead," he writes, when the sense is keenest
of the awful tragedy that makes him a marked man. But
in writing to Coleridge he was generally in a sportive vein.
"What do you think of smoking?" he says. "I want your
sober, average, noon opinion on it. . . . Morning is a
girl, and can't smoke—she's no evidence one way or the
other ; and Night is so evidently *bought over* that he
can't be a very upright judge. May be the truth is, that
one pipe is wholesome ; *two* toothsome ; *three* pipes
noisome ; *four* pipes fulsome ; *five* pipes quarrelsome,
and that's the *sum* on't. . . . Bless you, old sophist, who
next to human nature taught me all the corruption I was
capable of knowing, . . . when shall we two smoke
again ? " Can it be that much of this, and such as this,
was but the motley in which his great sorrow was pleased
to masquerade ? Lamb and his sister visited Coleridge
at Greta Hall in the summer of 1802. " Coleridge had
got a blazing fire in his study," writes Lamb in August,
" which is a large, antique, ill-shaped room with an old-
fashioned organ never played upon, big enough for a
church, shelves of scattered folios, an Eolian harp, and
an old sofa, half bed." The Lambs seem to have
enjoyed themselves greatly. The old schoolfellows
added to their other accomplishments that of inimitable
punsters. Lamb's puns got some additional effect from
the impediment in his speech ; Coleridge's were more
humorous than witty. For three weeks these old cronies
of the " Salutation and Cat " punned and smoked.
Lamb had grown pot-valiant in the art of smoking since

they smoked herbs mildly mixed with oronokoo in the smoky tavern in Newgate Street, and Coleridge had gone through the memorable ordeal at Birmingham, and the smoky process of learning German in Germany. Lamb and his sister went home early in September. "Mary is a good deal fatigued," Lamb writes, "and finds the difference in going *to* a place, and coming *from* it. I feel that I shall remember your mountains to the last day I live. They haunt me perpetually. I am like a man who has been falling in love unknown to himself, which he finds out when he leaves the lady."

Coleridge's health and spirits seem to have been moderately good during these early years at Keswick. There is a story which shows both his readiness in *repartee* and his high animal spirits about this period. He was staying a few days with two friends at a farmhouse, when it was agreed to go to a horse race in the neighbourhood. The farmer provided horses for the party—good ones for the poet's two friends, and for Coleridge, whose shortcomings as a horseman were known, a small, bony, angular, slow, spiritless creature in a dirty bridle and with rusty stirrups. The three mounted and set off. Coleridge was soon left far behind. He was dressed that day in a black coat with black breeches, black silk stockings, and shoes. In this suit of woe he and his cuddy nicknamed a horse went jogging along until they were met by a long-nosed gentleman in a sporting costume. The sportsman's nose quivered, and he stopped. "Pray, sir," he said, with a mighty knowing twinkle, "did you meet a tailor along the road?" "A tailor?" "Yes, a tailor; do you see, sir, he rode just such a horse as you ride, and for all the

world was just like you!" "Oh, oh," said Coleridge,
"I *did* meet a person answering such a description, who
told me that he had dropped his goose, that if I rode a
little farther I should find it; and I guess by the arch-
fellow's looks, he must have meant you!" "Caught a
tartar," said the long-nosed sportsman, and he rode off
smartly. So Coleridge jogged on again, like Parson
Adams on a donkey, until he came to the racecourse,
and there he drew up by a barouche and four, containing
a baronet (a member of Parliament), and several smart
ladies, and sundry gorgeous flunkeys. "A pretty piece
of blood, sir, you have there," said the baronet, with a
curl of the upper lip. "Yes," said Coleridge. "Rare
paces, I have no doubt." "Yes, he brought me here a
matter of four miles an hour." "Will you sell him?"
"Yes." "Name your price—rider and all." The ladies
began to titter. "My price for the *horse*, sir, is one
hundred guineas—as to the *rider*, never having been in
parliament, *his* price is not yet fixed." The baronet had
enough.

Coleridge at this period was a man of great animal
spirits, and (strange as it may sound) of extraordinary
physical energy. Writing to Wedgewood, January 9, 1803,
he gives a most interesting and surprising picture of his
vigour as a mountaineer. "I write," he says, "with
difficulty, with all the fingers but one of my right hand
very much swollen. Before I was half up the *Kirkstone*
mountain, the storm had wetted me through and through,
and before I reached the top it was so wild and out-
rageous, that it would have been unmanly to have suffered
the poor woman (guide) to continue pushing on, up

against such a torrent of wind and rain : so I dismounted and sent her home with the storm in her back.   I am no novice in mountain mischiefs, but such a storm as this was, I never witnessed, combining the intensity of the cold with the violence of the wind and rain.   The rain drops were pelted or slung against my face by the gusts, just like splinters of flint, and I felt as if every drop cut my flesh.   My hands were all shrivelled up like a washerwoman's, and so benumbed that I was obliged to carry my stick under my arm.   O, it was a wild business !   Such hurry skurry of clouds, such volleys of sound !   In spite of the wet and the cold, I should have had some pleasure in it, but for two vexations; first, an almost intolerable pain came into my right eye, a smarting and burning pain ; and secondly, in conse-quence of riding with such cold water under my seat, extremely uneasy and burthensome feelings attacked my groin, so that, what with the pain from the one and the alarm from the other, I had *no enjoyment at all !*   Just at the brow of the hill I met a man dismounted, who could not sit on horse-back.   He seemed quite scared by the uproar, and said to me, with much feeling, ' O sir, it is a perilous buffeting, but it is worse for you than for me, for I have it at my back.'   However I got safely over, and immediately all was calm and breathless, as if it was some mighty fountain put on the summit of Kirkstone, that shot forth its volcano of air, and precipi-tated huge streams of invisible lava down the road to Patterdale.   I went on to Grasmere."

Again (Jan. 14, 1803), he writes, "You ask me ' Why, in the name of goodness, I did not return when I saw the state of the weather?' The true reason is simple, though it may be somewhat strange. The thought never once entered my head. The cause of this I suppose to be, that (I do not remember it at least) I never once in my whole life turned back in fear of the weather. Prudence is a plant of which I no doubt possess some valuable specimens, but they are always in my hothouse, never out of the glasses, and least of all things would endure the climate of the mountains. In simple earnestness, I never find myself alone, within the embracement of rocks and hills, a traveller up an alpine road, but my spirit careers, drives, and eddies, like a leaf in autumn ; a wild activity of thoughts, imaginations, feelings, and impulses of motion rises up from within me ; a sort of bottom wind, that blows to no point of the compass, comes from I know not whence, but agitates the whole of me ; my whole being is filled with waves that roll and stumble, one this way, and one that way, like things that have no common master. I think that my soul must have pre-existed in the body of a chamois chaser. The simple image of the old object has been obliterated, but the feelings, and impulsive habits, and incipient actions, are in me, and the old scenery awakens them."

The Coleridge depicted in these letters is not the Coleridge of much biography and criticism, but it is unquestionably the Coleridge of reality. Here is a companion portrait by Wordsworth :

" Within our happy Castle there dwelt one
        Whom without blame I may not overlook ;
    For never sun on living creature shone
        Who more devout enjoyment with us took :

Here on his hours he hung as on a book ;
On his own time here would he float away,
    As doth a fly upon a summer brook ;
But go to-morrow—or, belike, to-day—
Seek for him,—he is fled ; and whither none can say.

Thus often would he leave our peaceful home,
    And find elsewhere his business or delight ;
Out of our valley's limits did he roam :
    Full many a time upon a stormy night
    His voice came to us from the neighbouring height :
Oft did we see him driving full in view,
    At midday, when the sun was shining bright ;
What ill was on him, what he had to do,
A mighty wonder bred among our quiet crew."

Towards the end of 1802 Coleridge made a tour in
Wales with Thomas Wedgewood, whose health was
failing.   In 1803 he was much from home.   He visited
the Wedgewoods in London, Poole at Stowey, and
Southey at Bristol.   Southey's wife lost her only child
in the summer of this year, and in her sorrow she went off
to her sister at Keswick.   Southey accompanied her, and
forthwith pitched his tent there, sharing Greta Hall with
Coleridge and their landlady.   During the same summer
Coleridge made a tour into Scotland with Wordsworth
and his sister.   Wordsworth had married, in the previous
October, an old playfellow from Penrith, Mary Hutchinson.
Early in his residence at Grasmere he had published,
with his own name only, a second series of the "Lyrical
Ballads," through Longmans, who paid £100 for the
two volumes.   It does not appear that Coleridge shared
this sum, though the "Ancient Mariner" and some four

of his other poems were still included.[1]   The party were
not long together in Scotland.   They visited Burns's
grave, the Clyde, Loch Katrine, and the Trossachs.
Rogers met them in the course of the tour, "in a vehicle
that looked very like a cart."   The weather was wet and
dull, and Coleridge began to suffer from rheumatism.
Before long, he left the Wordsworths, and returned home
rather hastily.   "Poor Coleridge," Wordsworth wrote,
"was at that time in bad spirits, and somewhat too much
in love with his own dejection, and he departed from us."
Wordsworth was not often so much ruffled beneath his
calm exterior.   He loved Coleridge as a brother, and
generally spoke of him with brotherly affection.

And now we are at a point of the highest importance
in the record of Coleridge's life.   From the date of his
return from Scotland to Keswick, to nurse his rheumatism
and suppressed gout with the "Kendal Black Drop," the
current of his life takes a change.   He had hitherto been
a man of enormous mental activity and sufficient physical
energy.   His personal character had been sweet and
affectionate.   He was a man made to love, and to be
beloved.   His friends had been bound to him by hooks
of steel.   As husband and father he had shown infinite
love and tenderness, and even more anxiety for the
material welfare of his wife and children than the
vicissitudes of his career had justified.   All was peace
and love in his home.   He had worked hard and con-
tinuously, and produced an enormous body of work.
Some of it was the very highest of its order, and a little

[1] A year later Wordsworth offered Coleridge £100 to enable him
to go to Madeira in search of health.

of it was entirely alone of its kind. He had written and published two volumes of poetry, and had a third volume in manuscript. He had produced as much journalistic work as would fill four good-sized volumes. He had lectured frequently, and preached times without number. He had spent a year in continental travel, had learned a new language, and translated a great play. He had written a noble tragedy. At thirty-one years of age he had attained to a distinct reputation. Who shall say that thus far he had shown any deficiency in moral force, or worldly wisdom, or common-sense? He had done the long day's work of a giant, and never lost a chance that any of his best friends would have valued. Let no one talk of him as if he were an inspired imbecile, on any evidence that these first thirty-one years supply! Down to this period he was a strong man, strongly equipped, working well against great odds, and moderately successful.

CHAPTER VIII.

COLERIDGE parted from the Wordsworths at
Tarbet late in August, 1803, and returning by
Edinburgh, he reached Keswick about the 1st of September. He seems to have taken to his bed immediately,
and to have been confined to it, with intervals of
convalescence, during the following six months. His
complaint was rheumatism and gout, complicated by
other disorders. He attributed his condition partly
to the chronic effects of the boyish indiscretion from
which he had suffered while at school — that of
swimming the New River in his clothes—partly to the
constant rains and his frequent drenchings in Scotland,
and partly to the prevailing humidity of the climate in
which he had made his permanent abode. While he lay
in bed he formed various designs of going abroad, sometimes to the West Indies, sometimes to the Canary
Islands, sometimes to Italy. Meantime he was his own
doctor. In youth he had read numerous books on
medicine, and now in the library of his neighbour and
landlord at Greta Hall there were, unhappily, many
medical reviews and magazines to which in his extremity
he resorted. "I had always," he says, "a fondness (a

common case, but most mischievous turn with reading
men who are at all dyspeptic) for dabbling in medical
writings; and in one of these reviews I met a case which
I fancied very like my own, in which a cure had been
effected by the ' Kendal Black Drop.' In an evil hour
I procured it: it worked miracles—the swellings disappeared, the pains vanished; I was all alive, and all
around me being as ignorant as myself, nothing could
exceed my triumph. I talked of nothing else, prescribed
the newly-discovered panacea for all complaints, and
carried a bottle about with me, not to lose any opportunity of administering 'instant relief and speedy cure' to
all complainers, stranger or friend, gentle or simple."
The illness had been a very real thing. In November,
Southey, now resident at Greta Hall, wrote: "Coleridge
is now in bed with the lumbago. Never was poor fellow
tormented with such pantomimic complaints; his disorders are perpetually shifting, and he is never a week
together without some one or other." Again, a month
or two later, Southey wrote, "Coleridge is quacking
himself for complaints that would tease anybody into
quackery." The panacea was not so real. "Need I
say," says Coleridge, "that my own apparent convalescence was of no longer continuance; but what
then?—the remedy was at hand and infallible. Alas!
it is with a bitter smile, a laugh of gall and bitterness,
that I recall this period of unsuspecting delusion, and
how I first became aware of the maelstrom, the fatal
whirlpool, to which I was drawing just when the current
was already beyond my strength to stem." The infallible
"Kendal Black Drop" turned out to be little else than

the very fallible opium, and it was thus, as a relief from pain, in ignorance, and as a victim of medical solecism, that Coleridge first came under the dreadful yoke of opium-eating. At what period the "Kendal Black Drop" was superseded by laudanum does not appear. That date, if it could be ascertained, would at least possess the melancholy interest of fixing the time at which the plea of error was fully overthrown, and the withering vice became chargeable to infirmity of purpose. Before this, the daily indulgence in narcotics had probably ceased to be entirely an act of free will and intention, but the full moral responsibility only began when the veil of ignorance was removed.

Coleridge had recovered from physical prostration early in 1804, and in April of that year a friend, John Stoddart, invited him to Malta. It was the opportunity he had longed for, and he accepted the offer. He insured his life, and set out early in April, going by way of London, where he "dined and punched" with Lamb. He arrived at Malta on April 18th, and on the 22nd he had a partial relapse. "I was reading when I was taken ill, and felt an oppression of my breathing, and convulsive snatching in my stomach and limbs." In this relapse there was, of course, but one resource—opium—and Coleridge resorted to it. He rallied, and found himself relieved by the climate and the stimulus of change ; but the summer came quickly, and then the dead summer heat, and the monotonous blue sky acted as a sedative, and he began to realize that his health did not improve. His limbs were "as lifeless tools," and the pains in his stomach became yet more violent and convulsive. To opium again and again he turned for relief from suffering. He had travelled chiefly in the interests of health ; but when the Governor of the island, Sir Alexander Ball, offered him a temporary post as public secretary, he accepted it. The duties were light and by no mean disagreeable, but the condition of his health often made them irksome. There appears to have been some pomp attaching to the office, and Coleridge prayed to be relieved from the unnecessary parade and dignity. The simplicity of his manners is said to have made him an object of curiosity in Malta, and to have given rise to whimsical stories. He did not find much to admire in the Maltese. "What can Sir Francis Head mean," he says, " by talking of the musical turn of the Maltese ? Why, when I was at Malta all nature was discordant. The very cats caterwauled more horribly and pertinaciously there than I ever heard elsewhere. The children will stand and scream inarticulately at each other for an hour together, out of pure love of dissonance. The dogs are deafening,—and so throughout. Musical, indeed ! I have hardly gotten rid of the noise yet ! " He describes the moral corruption of the Maltese when the island was surrendered. A marquis of an ancient family applied to the Governor to be appointed his valet. The marquis explained that he hoped that in the desired capacity he might have the honour of presenting petitions to his Excellency. " Oh, that is it, is it ? " said the Governor. " My valet, sir, brushes my clothes and brings them to me. If he dared to meddle with matters of public business, I should kick him downstairs." Coleridge did not make the best of business men, but he is said to have

been an able diplomatic writer in the department of correspondence. He gives us some amusing accounts of how
he figured as a magistrate. Towards September, 1805,
Coleridge resigned his public secretaryship. His friends
were then anxiously looking out for his return. "We
have lately built on our little rocky orchard," writes Wordsworth, "a little circular hut, lined with moss like a wren's
nest, and Coleridge has never seen it. What a happiness it would be to see him here !" During this summer
Thomas Wedgewood had died, but from fear of its effects
on her husband's health, Mrs. Coleridge kept back the
announcement. When Coleridge left Malta he did not
return to England, but went on a Government commission to Sicily. Later in the year he visited Rome, and
there made the acquaintance of Allston, the American
painter; Tieck, the German poet; and Humboldt, the
Prussian minister at the Papal Court. He was in Rome
about eight months, and left rather suddenly in August,
1806. He had intended to pass through Switzerland and
Germany to England, but from this route he was dis-
suaded by Humboldt, who told him that he was a marked
man; that unless he took care to keep himself unknown
while within the reach of Buonaparte, he might end his
career in the Temple at Paris. It leaked out that Coleridge had made himself obnoxious to the First Consul
by an article written for *The Morning Post.* In this
predicament he had a visit one morning from a Bene-
dictine,[1] who brought a passport signed by the Pope,
left a carriage, and admonished him to take to instant
flight. Coleridge obeyed. Reaching Leghorn he found

[1] Said to be Cardinal Fesch.

an American vessel ready to set sail for England. It is said that on the voyage they were chased by a French vessel, and that Coleridge was compelled to throw his papers overboard. The statement is a little doubtful. "After a most miserable passage from Leghorn of fifty-five days," he writes, "during which my life was twice given over, I found myself again in my native country, ill, penniless, and worse than homeless."

Worse than homeless! The startling words bear but one interpretation. They cannot mean that by reason of poverty he and his family were practically without a home. His wife and children were still at Greta Hall, living on his Wedgewood pension of £150 a year. He meant now what he had meant eleven years before, when he said that he was most a stranger in his native place. He pointed to an estrangement which made him worse than homeless, because in name he still had a home. What was the cause of this estrangement, and when did it arise? The entire subject is enshrouded in mystery, and we can only draw our inferences as to what the facts must have been. Coleridge had been more than two years out of England. He left home on good terms with his wife and his wife's relations. He was then ill in body and depressed in mind. On the day after he sailed Southey wrote, "Coleridge is gone for Malta, and his departure affects me more than I let be seen." Could words indicate with more certainty the love and sympathy which was felt for Coleridge by those whom he left at home? Southey felt it a duty to support the sinking spirits of wife and sister by concealing the emotion that came of Coleridge's departure under melancholy conditions. An idea of a sad and speedy end was constantly present to the minds of the people at Greta Hall. "The tidings of his death," says Southey, "would come upon me more like a stroke of lightning than any evil I have yet endured." So they waited eagerly at Keswick for the first news that should give hint of an improved condition. A letter came saying that he was worse rather than better. Then, after an interval, another letter described his official appointment. This intelligence must have been of the nature of a baffling difficulty. How Coleridge could undertake the duties of a public office, and yet be as ill as he described, was more than wife and family could comprehend at a distance of thousands of miles from the scene. At longer intervals other letters were received, all unsatisfactory as to matters of fact, all indefinite as to ultimate intentions. At length there came the announcement that the secretaryship had been resigned. Wife, family, and friends were then looking out for Coleridge's return. Probably he led them to expect it. But instead of returning he went yet farther afield, and then amid bewildering uncertainty all correspondence was stopped. From August, 1805, when he was on the point of leaving Malta, to May, 1806, Coleridge did not write one letter home. "No news from Coleridge of a later date than August." "No news from Coleridge," Wordsworth writes more than once. There is great anxiety as to his safety. Is he alive? Or has that sudden death which Southey foresaw overtaken him in a strange country? Letters written from Keswick do not reach him; but this fact is not yet known. Then it is heard indirectly that Coleridge is living

in Rome.   At that point the whole current of feeling at
Greta Hall undergoes a change.   Coleridge is indifferent
to their suspense.   They are wasting anxiety on one who
troubles himself little, or not at all, to relieve them.   " I
have no doubt whatever," says Southey, " that the reason
why we receive no letters is that he writes none; when
he comes he will probably tell a different story, and it
will be proper to admit his excuse without believing it."
The inference has been a bitter pill to the family at
Keswick, but they have felt compelled to swallow it.

So much for the posture of affairs at Greta Hall.   What
about Coleridge's position ?   Before he left home in
April, 1804, he was a shattered man.   His bodily health
had been reduced by six months' confinement to bed, and
his mental health had suffered a more serious overthrow.
He had realized that his free will had been sapped away,
and that he had lost the government of the commonest
acts of life.   Too late, as he believed, to regain self-
command, he had come to know that he was under the
yoke of opium.   It was a sordid slavery, and his great
soul learned its fullest bitterness.   " I have never been
capable of saying No," he wrote at one period.   Now he
found to his great horror that he could least of all say
" No " to himself.   His friends wished him to try the
effects of a foreign climate, and he was willing to go
abroad ; but he left home with the secret certainty that
whatever good the stimulus of change might do to his
bodily health under fair conditions, his moral strength
and intellectual spontaneity were already reduced below
the power of recuperation.   Coleridge did not bid farewell
to his wife and children with that sad pleasure which comes

to the man who, parting from his dear ones in sickness
and depression, looks through a mist of tears to that day
in the near future when he shall rejoin them in health
and spirits.   It was a half-hopeless errand, and the man
who undertook it was brought very low in his own esteem.
He loved wife and children with a passionate love, but
he could no longer think of them with pride, for the
source of pride was dry.   In his own eyes he was an
abject thing.   He could not write now to wife and child
as he wrote in the brave days of the jaunt in Germany,
" My dear, dear love ! and my Hartley ! my blessed
Hartley ! "   No longer had he a right to such words of
proud endearment.   A slave, a sordid slave, groaning
daily and hourly under a yoke that he had himself
hung about his neck—what a thing he was in his
own eyes !   And what if they who loved him in the
ignorance of compassion only knew the truth !   How
their hearts would turn from him !   How their adora-
tion would change to contempt, and their sympathy
to loathing !   And so in an agony of self-reproach
Coleridge was silent.   Every letter brought pain in the
degree in which it showed trust and love.

Then came the time when he was free to return to
England.   But why should he go back ?   He was not
better in bodily health, but worse, and his moral slavery
was yet more abject than before.   Still he must move,
for the restless spirit of discontent had to be appeased.
Let it be anywhere, anywhere but home, where the eyes
of love would surely peer into his secret and read his
shame.   So Coleridge took the first chance of removing
to Rome.   With that step his humiliation reached its

climax. Had he not confessed to himself by a deliberate act that he was the victim of a sinful infirmity? It was an infirmity that made the father childless. Self-pride could bear up no longer, and Coleridge cut off all connection with his home. Better that he should die unknown in a strange country than that he should live to hide his weakness in duplicity, or reveal his miserable sufferings to those whose eyes looked up to him. An accident hastened his departure from Rome, and the uncertain feet of the wanderer turned towards England. "I found myself again in my native country, ill, penniless, and worse than homeless."

He went back to Keswick. There he encountered many anxious looks, and perhaps some expostulations, and he could bear neither the one nor the other. Why had he not written during the whole period of a year? Had he no thought for wife and children? Nay, why had he gone on to Rome to live for nine or ten months on the earnings of a previous year? Coleridge could find no peace in his home. He was not understood there. What remained to him of proper pride was now as much wounded by the misrepresentation of his wife as formerly by the misrepresentation of his mother and brothers. Mrs. Coleridge was a worthy, practical-minded woman, without much intellectual insight. Perhaps she realized that her husband was a man of large gifts and attainments. More probably she took this knowledge in trust from others, who paid Coleridge obvious homage. In any case such superiority could only have value in her eyes if

---

[1] A lady who knew Mrs. Coleridge tells me that she was "a fine woman, but a rather fidgety body."

it led to material results. It did not lead to material results, and her wifely pride was humiliated by constant observation of Southey's substantial success. Coleridge, on his part, must leave his home. He was distressed by his wife's misunderstanding, and rebuked by his own accusing conscience. In the presence of daily evidence of Southey's growing fame he was probably as unhappy in his own way as his wife would be in hers. He had ties to bind him to home. There were four of his children now at Greta Hall, and many a sweet idyll of childhood held the tender-hearted man with hooks of steel; his little Sara plucking plums from trees in their dotage in a worn-out orchard, and her little cousin Edith swinging from a bough of an apple-tree; his little Derwent announcing that he had been made by James Lawson, the Keswick carpenter, out of " the stuff he makes wood of," and that James had " sawed him off," and that " he didn't like it." But Coleridge could not bear either mis- directed reproaches, or the sight of the happiness which he had forfeited the right to claim.

In his misery he turned to the friend who was dearest of all men to him—the friend to whom he was dearest. Wordsworth had gone to Coleorton, the seat of their new friend, Sir George Beaumont, a painter, better known as the friend and patron of painters. So Coleridge went down to Coleorton, and was received with a pathetic warmth of sympathy, but even there a new form of suffering awaited him. Wordsworth read the poem now called "The Prelude," and Coleridge listened to it in raptures. But the second sense was one of pain. What had he himself been doing while his friend had accomplished work like this? Nearly ten years had passed since they rambled together over the Quantock Hills and discussed the new school of poetry which was to vivify common incidents with the light of imagination, and do for the events of daily life what a sudden gleam of moonlight does for a familiar landscape. Since then he had done little or nothing that was worthy of his great powers. Seven of those ten years had been filled with the drudgery of journalism ; three had been utterly thrown away. If he had felt himself to be "a little man" beside Wordsworth in those old days, he had not felt that he was therefore any the less in relation to other men. But now even this poor unction was gone. He *was* a little man beside other men, because he was one who of weakness and wantonness had stunted his own faculties. The dark column of hope which in those days was not yet fully turned had turned again, and now all was hopeless darkness. The night after the reading of "The Prelude" Coleridge wrote these lines :

> " O great Bard !
> Ere yet that last strain dying awed the air,
> With steadfast eye I view'd thee in the choir
> Of ever-enduring men. . . .
> Ah ! as I listened with a heart forlorn,
> The pulses of my being beat anew."

What did Wordsworth think of the change in Coleridge? If we turn to the "Stanzas written in my pocket copy of Thomson's ' Castle of Indolence,' " we may see how that change affected him. The poem has a touch of mystery which was probably introduced as a cover for the hard facts ; but there can scarcely be a doubt that Coleridge, the man and the poet, Coleridge in his days of hope and of depression, is in the eye of the poet.

> "Ah ! piteous sight it was to see this man
> When he came back to us a withered flower,
> Or, like a sinful creature, pale and wan.
> Down would he sit ; and without strength or power
> Look at the common grass from hour to hour." [1]

[1] Mr. Dowden, in his "Life of Shelley," identifies William Calvert, the friend of Coleridge and Shelley, as the second of the two dwellers in Wordsworth's "Castle of Indolence." A baffling difficulty in accepting Mr. Dowden's theory comes to me from my friend Mr. Edwin Jackson (Hawthorns, Keswick), who has discovered that Calvert could not have been the "noticeable man with large grey eyes," (1) because his eyes were not grey, but very dark ; (2) because the poem says that the people of the valley wondered what business the noticeable man could have among them, whereas Calvert had the very obvious business of one who came of a family that had for two centuries occupied a position of almost the highest local interest. In the families of the Wordsworths, the Coleridges, and the Calverts, the idea has always had a silent acceptance that Coleridge alone was meant ; but that any reader of the sixth and seventh stanzas of Wordsworth's poem could apply them to Coleridge is at least sufficiently surprising. It must be allowed, however, that the description in the fifth stanza is a close parallel to Dorothy Wordsworth's description of Coleridge. I find it no less difficult to accept the theory favoured by Mr. W. Knight and Mr. F. W. H. Myers, that Wordsworth was describing himself in the lines I have quoted. So far as it concerns Coleridge, the question is open to an easy solution. If Wordsworth's poem was written in 1802, exactly as published in 1815, then Coleridge cannot be identified as either of the two men. It was not until 1806 that Coleridge returned to England as a shattered man.

CHAPTER IX.

WHEN Wordsworth and Coleridge published the first series of " Lyrical Ballads " at Bristol, there was a lad of fourteen at school in Bath who was fascinated by " The Ancient Mariner." Four years later, when the poets were making their tour in Scotland, the lad was living the life of an outcast in London, having escaped from school and the tyranny of his guardians. He was Thomas De Quincey, son of a merchant who had died when Thomas was a child. From the poverty of his lodgings in Soho he was rescued by his friends, and sent at eighteen as a student to Oxford. This was in 1803, and he remained at the University down to 1808. In the meantime he had made frequent visits to London, and there he had contracted the friendship of Charles Lamb. His admiration of Coleridge had increased since his schoolboy days, and his interest in the poet was crowned when he learned in 1804 that the author of the "Ancient Mariner" was applying his mind to the student's own pursuits—metaphysics and psychology. Above all things he wished for personal knowledge of so original a genius, and on hear-

ing in 1805 that Coleridge was residing in Malta as
Secretary to the Governor, he began to inquire about the
best route to the island.　But the times were turbulent,
and any route promised the young enthusiast an inside
place in a French prison.　So he was reconciled to waiting, until, in 1807, he heard that Coleridge was not only
in England, but within measurable distance of the place
at which he was then visiting.　Without losing an hour
he bent his steps towards Nether Stowey, where Coleridge was understood to be staying with his friend
Thomas Poole.　At length he encountered the poet in
the street at Bridgewater.

Coleridge took the young man to the house of his
host, and there, in the midst of conversation, the door
opened, and a lady entered.　" She was in person full,
and rather below the middle height," says De Quincey,
"while her face showed, to my eye, some prettiness of
rather a commonplace order."　Coleridge paused on the
lady's entrance, and turning to his visitor, said in a frigid
tone, " Mrs. Coleridge."　De Quincey bowed, the lady
acknowledged the introduction, and immediately retired.
The scene was short and ungenial, and De Quincey
learned from it that Coleridge's marriage was not a
happy one.　It is neither necessary nor desirable to enter
into his subsequent explanations of the causes of the
supposed mésalliance.　His record of facts is obviously
untrustworthy, and the inferences he draws from it
sufficiently prove that this man of extraordinary genius
was deficient in knowledge of human nature.　When he
sets aside his poor tattle about Mrs. Coleridge's jealousy
of Miss Wordsworth, and comes to the clear fact of Cole-

ridge's personal wretchedness, and to the explanation that Coleridge gave of the unhappy overclouding of his life, we have a strong sense of the truthfulness of the narrative. De Quincey remarked accidentally that he had been obliged to take a few drops of laudanum for toothache, and thereupon Coleridge made confession of his own habit of opium eating, and warned him with all the emphasis of horror against forming a habit of the same kind. Coleridge gave De Quincey the impression that he never hoped to liberate himself from the bondage. "My belief is that he never *did*," says De Quincey. Many years afterwards Coleridge made a note of the same conversation. "Oh, may the God to whom I look for mercy through Christ," he writes, "show mercy on the author of the 'Confessions of an Opium Eater,' if, as I have too strong reason to believe, his book has been the occasion of seducing others into the withering vice through wantonness. From this aggravation I have, I humbly trust, been free, as far as acts of my free will and intention are concerned; even to the author of that work I pleaded with flowing tears and with an agony of forewarning. He utterly denied it, but I fear that I had even then to *deter*, perhaps not to forewarn." We know now that Coleridge and De Quincey were both in error as to the facts.

When De Quincey met Mrs. Coleridge at Bridgewater, she with three of her children had left Keswick in the hope of settling with her husband at Bristol. In February, 1807, Southey writes : "Mrs. Coleridge and her children are to join Coleridge early in April, and go into Devonshire, where the longer they stay the better. Perhaps, if

Wordsworth settles in the South, they will not return
at all, which is what I wish, as it would tempt me
hugely to fix here." Whatever the scheme was that had
suggested Bristol, it came to nothing. De Quincey did
Coleridge a two-fold service at this juncture. Con-
ceiving that his depression arose in part from pecuniary
embarrassments, he presented him secretly, through
Cottle, with three hundred pounds;[1] and on the final
abandonment of the intention to settle at Bristol, he
took Mrs. Coleridge and her children back to Keswick.
Some time later Southey writes : " Mrs. Coleridge takes
on herself poor Jackson's house," a portion of Greta Hall,
" in expectation that Coleridge will one day come back ;
and still more because he will have a place to which he
may come whenever he likes, as if it were his own house
—a thing which cannot be with my establishment, ought
not and shall not." "How *cold* he is," as Wordsworth
said of Southey. His words are bitterly cruel. What
do they mean ? Are we to understand that Southey, a
heavily burdened man, had all these years been bearing
the burdens of Coleridge also ? If that is a fair inference,
the words are not only cruel, but false. Greta Hall had

---

[1] Writing to Cottle from Calne, March 7, 1815, Coleridge says,
"Heaven knows, of the £300 received through you, what went to
myself." Cottle thereupon refers the disappearance of so large a
sum to opium debts. "Mr. C. lived with his friends, and he could
contract few other debts." There is no sufficient evidence that
Coleridge ever "lived" at the expense of any friend. At the time
alluded to by Cottle, he was living rent free at the office of *The
Courier*, but he was paying for his own board. At Morgan's,
from 1811 to 1814, and at Gillman's, from 1816 to 1834, he paid
for board and lodgings.

been rented by Coleridge in 1800. Three years afterwards Southey joined him and shared the rent. In 1807
Southey undertook the whole of that part of the house
which was not occupied by the landlord. From April,
1807, to January, 1810, Mrs. Coleridge and her children
lodged with Southey, paying for their maintenance out of
the permanent Wedgewood pension of £150, every penny
of which was appropriated to their sole use.[1] Then, the
landlord being dead, Mrs. Coleridge took his share of
Greta Hall, mainly in order that her husband might have
a home of his own to come to, and not be deterred from
returning to his wife and children by any thought of the
cheerless lodgings let out to him by the dear brother-in-
law who had superseded him. Let us be quite just to
Southey. No doubt he was often sorely tried by those
weaknesses of Coleridge, which, as we now see, he never
for one instant understood. No man who came so close
to Coleridge, so frequently and so painfully misunderstood
him. The two men were cast in entirely different moulds,
and had not one angle of resemblance. In character, in
habits, in morals and mind, they were completely unlike.
An accident brought them together; a kindred enthusiasm made them friends; marriage made them relatives,
and brought them beneath one roof. In early years they
bore one another a sincere affection, for each had qualities
the other could admire. But when the days of sorrow
came, and the sufferer was silent as to the worst of his
sufferings, the casual friend, made relative and housemate,

---

[1] There are several authorities for this important statement. The
best to cite is the most hostile : Southey, writing to Cottle, April
17, 1814.

had no plummet wherewith to sound the deep places of the heart.[1]

On leaving the Wordsworths at Coleorton in the winter of 1806, Coleridge had come up to London and resumed journalism.   His friend Stuart had sold *The Morning Post*, but still retained a part proprietorship of *The Courier*, his partner being a journalist named Street.   Stuart found Coleridge penniless, and, to save expense, gave him apartments at the offices of *The Courier* in the Strand. Years afterwards Stuart altogether denied that Coleridge at this period rendered services to the paper by way of equivalent, and certainly the accommodation was hardly worth any return.   The single room — an attic which answered for bed and sitting-room—was in immediate proximity to the printing establishment, and much disturbed as a consequence.   Coleridge appears to have been without any regular attendance, except such as could be given by a certain Mrs. Brainbridge, probably the keeper of the house, who lived down three flights of stairs.   In 1807 or 1808, De Quincey called upon him daily in these quarters.

[1] There is abundant evidence that from 1806 onwards there was no love lost between Coleridge and Southey.   Writing to Cottle, in 1836, Southey said, " I know that Coleridge, at different times of his life, never let an opportunity pass of speaking ill of me."   This is how Southey returned good for evil : " Can you tell me anything of Coleridge ? " he writes, in October, 1814 ; " we know that he is with the Morgans, at Calne.   What is to become of him ?   He may find men who will give him board and lodgings for the sake of his conversation, but who will pay his other expenses.   He leaves his family to chance and charity."   Coleridge was at this time paying two pounds ten shillings per week for board and lodgings, and was working daily at his " Biographia Literaria."

"There did I often see the philosopher," he says, "with the most lugubrious of faces, invoking with all his might this uncouth name of 'Brainbridge,' each syllable of which he intoned [from the head of the stairs] with long-drawn emphasis, in order to overpower the hostile hubbub coming down from the creaking press and the roar from the Strand, which entered at all the front windows. 'Mistress Brainbridge! I say, Mistress Brainbridge!' was the perpetual cry." It was a forlorn condition. With no society to sustain his cheerfulness, Coleridge's spirits flagged, and he sank more than ever under the dominion of opium.

In the winter of 1806 he undertook, through the offices of Sir Humphry Davy, to deliver at the Royal Institution two courses of eight lectures on the fine arts. He was to receive £120, and the sum appears to represent his sole earnings at this period. The lectures were successful, and in the winter following he was engaged to deliver a further course on the English Poets, the fee to be about the same as before. The second course of lectures failed most painfully. In the interval Coleridge had indulged his weakness yet more deeply, so that he was at least *four* times unable to fulfil his engagements. Then came the dismissal of audience after audience. "On many of his lecture days," says De Quincey, "I have seen all Albemarle Street closed by a 'lock' of carriages filled with women of distinction, until the servants of the Institution or their own footmen advanced to the carriage door with the intelligence that Mr. Coleridge had been taken suddenly ill." The plea was at first received with concern, then with incredulity, and finally with disgust.

But when the lecturer appeared, he justified by only too painful evidences his excuse of illness. "His lips were baked with feverish heat," says De Quincey, "and often black in colour ; and in spite of the water which he continued drinking through the whole course of his lecture, he often seemed to labour under an almost paralytic inability to raise the upper jaw from the lower." It was natural that the lectures should reflect the lecturer's exhaustion. They were discontinued, perhaps at Coleridge's request, probably at the instance of the Committee of the Institution, and Coleridge received a reduced honorarium of £100.

He occupied off and on his forlorn attic in the premises of *The Courier* down to the summer of 1808, and then returned to the Lake country and settled, not with his family at Greta Hall, but with the Wordsworths at Grasmere. By this distinct and overt act, Coleridge expressed an unmistakable intention of living apart from his wife. While he was in London his purposes in that regard were uncertain, but with less than thirteen miles between them, and no requirements of work to keep them asunder, his wife could not mistake his intentions. Nevertheless there was a strange intercourse between the households at Allan Bank and Greta Hall. With Wordsworth, Coleridge paid a visit to Keswick in September. "Coleridge is arrived at last," Southey writes, "about half as big as the house. He came over with Wordsworth on Monday, and returned with him on Wednesday. His present scheme is to put the boys to school at Ambleside, and reside at Grasmere himself." It is pleasant to turn from Southey's acrid account of affairs at Greta Hall, to the sketch made by Coleridge's daughter Sara of a month she spent with her father at Allan Bank in the same autumn. She was then a child of six. "I slept with him," she says, "and he would tell me fairy tales when he came to bed at twelve or one o'clock." But she mars the idyl with this addition : "I think my dear father was anxious that I should learn to love him, and the Wordsworths and their children, and not cling so exclusively to my mother, and all around me at home. He was, therefore, much annoyed when on my mother's coming to Allan Bank, I flew to her and wished not to be separated from her any more."

There was abundant literary society in the Lake country at this period—Professor Wilson, at Elleray ; Charles Lloyd, at Brathay ; Southey, at Keswick ; Wordsworth, Coleridge, and De Quincey at Grasmere ; and, among lesser men, Dr. Watson, the Bishop of Llandaff, at Windermere. To these came Scott, Lamb, and Hazlitt at intervals. During one of his visits, Hazlitt painted the portraits of Coleridge and Wordsworth. The portrait of Coleridge was a fine picture, but that of Wordsworth represented a physiognomy so dismal, that one of the poet's friends exclaimed on seeing it—"At the gallows, deeply affected by his deserved fate, yet determined to die like a man." Hazlitt disappointed himself as a painter, and revenged his vanity by becoming a critic of the fine arts. This was the period when Edinburgh was making its great effort to break the literary supremacy of London. The young men who met in that 'ninth' flat in Buccleugh Place, which was the elevated residence of Mr. Jeffrey, maintained opinions a little too liberal for the dynasty of Mr. Dundas, but the political rebellion was not their object when they started *The Edinburgh Review* in 1802. Their sole aim was literary; Jeffrey and his coadjutors, Brougham and Sydney Smith, meant to dispute the ground with Aiken and his coadjutors, Coleridge, Southey, and others who are now forgotten. They were not long in making it apparent that the magazine, *The Monthly*, represented by Aiken, was what Coleridge called it, an *aiken-void;* and then it began to appear that their utmost energy must be put forth in resisting the little band of writers that had found a rallying-point in the Lake country. We know that they went to work with a will. Beginning with Southey, and going on to Wordsworth, they did their best to discredit the "whining and hypocritical writers," who were "known to haunt the lakes of Cumberland." "In so far as we know," said the northern critics, "there are but few persons of sober taste and cultivated judgment in their train." They came even closer home than this, and saw that "the greater part of men of improved and delicate taste" treated the "Lakists" "with contempt and derision." It does not appear that the poets were seriously perturbed. Probably they realized that the critics were doing them important services unawares. At all events, they went on with their work. Southey wrote "Kehama" and "Madoc"; Wordsworth wrote many noble sonnets, and kept a strong hand for his great poem, "The Excursion"; Coleridge was for the time lost to poetry, but he worked even harder now than before. Coleridge's habits were curious; he transformed the night into day, and lived chiefly by candle-light. He rose from two to four in the afternoon, and long after all other lights had disappeared in the cottages of the secluded vale, Coleridge's lamp was still burning. When the dales-men from the Wythburn valley were coming over the Dunmail Raise to their work in the early morning, Coleridge was retiring to bed. This irregularity probably means that he was still under the dominion of opium. Nevertheless, he gives some hint of improvement. " I have been enabled," he writes, " to reduce the dose to one sixth part of what I formerly took, and my general health and mental activity are greater than I have known them for years past."

At what was Coleridge working during this period of residence at Grasmere ? Early in 1809—some six or seven months after he had removed from London—he conceived the idea of starting a literary miscellany to be called *The Friend.* This periodical was to be quite unlike *The Watchman* in scheme and character. *The Friend* was to be an original journal of politics, philosophy, literature, and the fine arts, and not in any sense a register or record of passing events. The plan of Coleridge's miscellany differed as much from the plan of *The Edinburgh Review*, then seven years old, and the plan of the rival review, *The Quarterly*, then newly started, as from that of *The Watchman.* Arrangements were made for the printing ; a subscription list was obtained, and on June 1, 1809, *The Friend* was started. It ran through twenty-seven numbers, and came to an end early in 1810. "Never was anything so grievously mismanaged," says Southey ; and De Quincey gives a woful account of the general bemuddlement into which the affairs of the publication fell. It would certainly appear that the busi ness arrangements were deficient in despatch, and it is conceivable that Coleridge, who was never a proficient in monetary concerns, was even more than ordinarily handicapped in this regard when the double duty of editor and business manager devolved upon him. But it would be folly to follow De Quincey in his picturesque but not very accurate account of the causes that contributed to the failure. If it were allowed—it certainly ought not to be on such dubious evidence—that Coleridge was an utter child in all financial affairs, the fact would remain that he was living in hourly intercourse with Wordsworth, who was at least above suspicion of complete artlessness where money was in question. Wordsworth had a personal interest in *The Friend;* he contributed to it with his pen, and the friend whose sole hope of earning a livelihood was centred in its success was then domesticated under his roof. The simple truth is that Coleridge was harassed by the defalcations of subscribers, and the lukewarmness of friends, and that these causes of anxiety acting on the inevitable worries, risks, and losses of publishing enterprise, led to a speedy collapse. There is, therefore, no reason to go far in search of reasons why *The Friend* should have failed. Its rivals were numerous, powerful, and the reverse of poor. Coleridge was possessed of a hundred pounds at the utmost computation, his literary coadjutors were men who *could* not help him, and his rich admirers from Albemarle Street and elsewhere *would* not. Stuart, alone, seems to have done anything to keep *The Friend* alive.

Disappointed, depressed, more than before under the dominion of opium, Coleridge went back to his wife and children at Keswick in the summer of 1810. There he remained about five months, with distinct benefit to his health. "Coleridge has been with us for some time past," writes Mrs. Coleridge, "in good health, spirits, and humour, but *The Friend*, for some unaccountable reason, or for no reason at all, is utterly silent. This, you will easily believe, is matter of perpetual grief to me, but I am obliged to be silent on the subject, although ever uppermost in my thoughts ; but I am obliged to bear about a cheerful countenance, knowing as I do by sad experience that to expostulate, or even hazard one anxious look, would soon drive him hence." From this letter it is sufficiently clear, that Coleridge shared De Quincey's opinion that his wife was wanting in cordial appreciation, or indeed comprehension, of her husband's intellectual powers, and was, therefore, not a person with whom he could share the anxieties in which every friend was made to participate. The letter makes it no less obvious that, whatever the depth of her affection for her husband, Mrs. Coleridge was wishful to live at peace with him, and was willing to undergo in silence much suffering, and to support with patience a constrained cheerfulness, in order to keep him at her side. That her efforts failed was not a mark of cruelty on the part of Coleridge. Once for all, for good or for ill, the idea had fixed itself upon his mind that it was no longer possible for him to hope for domestic happiness ; that the vision of a happy home had sunk for ever ; and—

> " That names but seldom meet with Love,
>   And Love wants courage without a name."

When and how this idea was engendered, in what
degree it was a hallucination, and how far it came of a
morbid reality, we have already vaguely conjectured.　If
it were needful to say in a word or two to what the idea
was due, we should promptly attribute it, not to the
incompatibility pointed to by De Quincey, not to faults
of intellect or temper on Mrs. Coleridge's part, and not
to any lack of the domestic temperament in Coleridge
himself, but to the drug—" the accursed drug."

Coleridge left his home early in October, 1810, and
never again returned to it.

> " He loved no other place, and yet
> Home was no home to him."

His immediate purpose seems to have been that of
consulting Abernethy.　He came up to London with
Basil Montagu, having accepted the invitation of the
Chancery barrister to live in his house.　The connection
soon terminated in a rupture, brought about by a rather
trivial incident in which Coleridge had exercised with
some freedom the privileges of guestship.　He removed
to the house of his friends, the Morgans, at Hammersmith,
and remained there from November to the following
January.　Then he took lodgings in Southampton Build-
ings.　To be cast back upon himself was a condition
always full of temptation to Coleridge, and in his cheerless lodgings he took more than ordinary doses of the drug.
" I am a little, and only a little better at present," he
writes; "if it is possible, I shall put myself in the Hammersmith stage this evening, as I am not fit to be in lodgings
by myself.　In truth, I have had such a series of anxieties,

cruel disappointments, and sudden shocks from the first
week of my arrival in London, that any new calamity
suffices to overset me." He returned to the Morgans
on February 11, 1811, and spent the three years following at their house. The anxieties, disappointments, and
shocks alluded to in this letter were very real and by no
means imaginary. He had earned absolutely nothing
since the beginning of 1808, when he received one
hundred guineas for his second series of lectures at the
Royal Institution. Every farthing of this sum must have
been sunk in *The Friend*, and debts were still arising out
of that ill-fated venture. It was now February, 1811, and
after three profitless years, the unlucky man found himself confronted by two grievous misfortunes. The first
of these was a bill, which in equity was as much another
man's debt as his own. The second, was the withdrawal
by Josiah Wedgewood of his half of the pension of £150
a year. Some amount of mystery enshrouds the former
of these difficulties ; the latter is said to have been
Wedgewood's protest against Coleridge's neglect of his
family. It is more than probable that the two difficulties
are in effect one difficulty, involving one set of persons
only, and that Wedgewood was prompted rather by pique
at what he thought " benefits forgot," than by any impulse so illogical as that of punishing a man for neglecting
his wife and children by taking the bread out of their
mouths. If the alleged reason for Wedgewood's conduct
is the true one, he cancelled every obligation due to him
for his liberality in the past. There is now no sort of
doubt that Mrs. Coleridge and her children enjoyed the
full benefit of the Wedgewood pension from the first. That

Coleridge did not fulfil his half of their agreement was no sufficient ground on which Wedgewood could repudiate a responsibility voluntarily undertaken, on his part, and accepted with a distinct sacrifice of other permanent emolument on the part of Coleridge.

Penniless, broken-spirited, and now at forty a grey-haired man, Coleridge, the dreamer of great dreams, the author of "The Ancient Mariner" and of "Christabel," betook himself once more to his friend Stuart, the part-proprietor of *The Courier*. Stuart knew nothing about literature, and very little about journalism, except what he could learn at the publishing counter. He had bought *The Morning Post* in 1790, for £600, and sold it in 1803, for something like £25,000. Coleridge was the chief writer, if not the editor, during the short crucial period of the paper's prosperity, and he always claimed to have made its fortune. When he came to write his life he said this with sufficient emphasis. Stuart was then very angry, and remonstrated privately, but Coleridge did not yield. The newspaper proprietor submitted to the grave imputation of having earned money by an editor's brains, believing in his generous soul that perhaps Coleridge wished to excuse himself to his friends for having done so little, by saying that the prime of his manhood had been wasted in journalism, or else that he wished to establish a claim against Government for a pension. But when long years afterwards Coleridge's biographer repeated the charge, Stuart wrote in wrathful protest a series of letters which were meant to show that Coleridge had done little or nothing for either of his papers, and that he had paid the poet no less a sum than £700 for his slender

services. Stuart was a dunderheaded person, but he had
the faculty of perceiving on which side his bread was
buttered. Coleridge thought him a generous friend, and
often applied to him in his extremity. He applied to
him at this crisis of 1811. Stuart's partner, Street, was
editor of *The Courier* at this time. Street was an incapa-
ble journalist who made up for professional shortcomings
by the skill he had at catching a nod from lord this and
lord that. In his hands *The Courier* degenerated to a
very tool of ministers, and lick-spittle of people in power.
The paper was odious to the people, and odious to Coleridge, but, nevertheless, the poor bankrupt journalist—who
might have been at the head of *The Morning Post*, the
leading paper of the hour, if his lust of money had been a
match for his love of letters—went meekly to Stuart and
his partner, and begged employment. Street had no belief
in Coleridge ; perhaps he was too stupid to recognize his
abilities, probably he was too shrewd not to be jealous
of any footing that might be gained by a man who was
infinitely his superior. But Coleridge's ambition was
modest enough and to spare. What did he ask ? He
asked to be allowed to attend at *The Courier* office from
nine o'clock in the morning until two in the afternoon, to
condense the police, parliamentary, and similiar reports
that had appeared in the other newspapers, and to write
an occasional Note on the affairs of the day. By much
artful show of modesty—there is nothing like the pinch
of poverty for making the most artless nature artful—
Coleridge induced Street to consent. He was too eager
for employment to make any stipulation as to terms, and
he began his work forthwith. Rising about six every

morning, he breakfasted, and got into the stage at
Hammersmith at twenty minutes past seven, arriving in
the Strand at half-past eight.   This daily coaching to and
fro involved a grievous outlay of eighteen shillings a week
and Coleridge's earnings were probably about as large as
those of a third-rate clerk.   To save nine shillings a week
he walked home every night from the Strand to Hammersmith.   His wages were received in irregular sums of
£5, and £10, as his necessities required.   He worked
on ; he was so poor that he begged Stuart to let him
have his old copies of the day's papers when he had done
with them.   But his cup of humiliation was still not full.
Street, like the nincompoop he was, filled the paper with
any trivial news of the day to the exclusion of the articles
that Coleridge's spirit, not yet wholly crushed, prompted
him to write.   These articles fell day after day into a
chaos of other papers that lay buried beyond resurrection
in the editor's drawer.   Coleridge could be beaten down
no longer.   A rupture arose out of an article that had
been so altered at the bidding of a minister that it was
scarcely recognizable to its author as his own.   Coleridge left *The Courier*, but not until his poverty had
compelled him to undergo a long period of torture.[1]

In 1811–12 Coleridge delivered before the London
Philosophical Society a series of seventeen lectures on
Shakespeare and Milton.   These lectures were in part
preserved by the shorthand notes—long lost, and recovered after forty years—of Payne Collier.   They

[1] The story of Coleridge's connection with *The Courier* is now
told for the first time. (For authorities see Coleridge's letters to
Stuart.)

were greatly successful. There were usually about a hundred and fifty hearers, and among them were Byron, Lamb, Rogers, and Crabb Robinson. Coleridge possessed nearly every qualification that ensures success on the platform—a deep voice, deliberation, and extraordinary powers of extemporaneous speech. He had his vices as a lecturer, and chief of these was the vice of digression. When he was announced to lecture on the Nurse in "Romeo and Juliet," he discoursed with infinite circumlocution on parental love, and provoked from Lamb this pertinent comment: "Not so bad—he was to give us a lecture on the Nurse, and he has given us one in the *manner* of the Nurse." The course ended with *éclat* on January 27, 1812, the hall being crowded, and the lecture brilliant. Coleridge must have earned a substantial sum by these lectures. He required all he got to eke out the wages of his appointment as condenser of reports.

In 1813 better luck came to him. The play "Osorio," written at Sheridan's suggestion in 1797, lay for ten years at Drury Lane. The manager gave it no better attention than to make it the subject of a stupid joke. "Coleridge sent me a play, and in one scene (a cavern) the water was said to drip, drip, drip—in fact it was all *dripping*." Sheridan's *régime* at the national theatre was succeeded by that of a committee, of which Lord Byron, the reigning poetic favourite, was a member. Byron induced the new management to accept Coleridge's play, and it was brought out under the title of "Remorse." The play was warmly received, and had a long run of twenty nights.　Coleridge's earnings were large for those times, probably two or three hundred pounds.　Encouraged by this success, and prompted by Byron's advice,[1] Coleridge tried his hand at drama once more.　He wrote "Zapolya," in 1814–15, but it was declined both at Drury Lane and at Covent Garden.　It had no parts for Miss O'Neil or Mr. Kean.

In this year, 1813, Coleridge went down to Bristol with the intention of re-delivering, under the management of his old friend, Joseph Cottle, the series of lectures which had been given with such acceptance before the London Philosophical Society.　He did not repeat his success.　Remaining at Bristol until the middle of 1814, he made more than one attempt at a course of lectures.　It is not recorded that he broke faith with his audiences, except in the case of an opening lecture, of which Cottle tells a silly and incredible story on hearsay.　His health was utterly broken.　So shattered were his nerves that he could not take up a glass of water without spilling it, though one hand supported the other.　It was a relapse to the condition of the winter 1807–8, and it was due to the same cause —the drug, the drug, always the accursed drug!　He was in the toils of his temptation, and his genial and generous nature grew suspicious and morose.　He set traps to defeat his weakness.　A man was engaged to follow him about the streets of Bristol in order to prevent him from buying laudanum at any chemist's shop that he might pass.　He despised himself for his

---

[1] Byron's advice was accompanied by the substantial benefit of the loan, early in 1815, of a hundred pounds.

infirmity ; he spent long nights in agonizing prayer for forgiveness in respect of the talents he abused. Then came the craving of the appetite to defeat remorse and overcome fortitude. "Before God," he cries, "I have but one voice—Mercy, mercy! woe is me. Pray for me that I may not pass such another night as the last. While I am awake and retain my reasoning powers the pang is gnawing, but I am, except for a fitful moment or two, tranquil ; it is the howling wilderness of sleep that I dread." It was a terrible conflict. No struggle more awful ever played a part in the life of any man. That fearful conflict day by day, night by night, between remorse and appetite—the heartrending appeals for mercy and forgiveness for genius wasted, the anguish of powerlessness, the sense of extinguished vigour, the thought of what might have been, and is not, and never can be—these are depths of suffering that we may not and should not sound. In such an awful crisis of all that is best in it and all that is worst, the naked soul should stand before God alone.

> " Life's ocean, breaking round thy senses' shore,
>   Struck golden song as from the strand of day."
>   THEODORE WATTS.

In 1814 Coleridge went to Calne, where his friend Morgan was now living in reduced circumstances. He was to pay two pounds ten shillings a week for board, lodgings, and etceteras. At Calne he wrote the "Biographia Literaria." He came back to London in 1816, and took lodgings at a chemist's laboratory in Norfolk Street. "Nature who conducts every creature, by instinct, to its end," says Lamb, "might as well have sent a *helluo librorum* for cure to the Vatican. God keep him inviolate among the traps and pitfalls !" Coleridge sank lower and lower. "Had I but a few hundred pounds, but £200," he had written, "half to send to Mrs. Coleridge, and half to place myself in a private madhouse, where I could procure nothing but what a physician thought proper, . . . then *there* might be hope. Now there is none." But there *was* hope, and the hope came, whence it might have been least expected, from the slave himself. Early in 1816 Coleridge put himself under the care of Dr. Gillman, of the Grove, Highgate, and took up his residence in the doctor's house. From that time dated the beginnings of his emancipation. It was a slow and gradual liberation, but it was complete at length. Long, painful, and toilsome years had passed before the slave threw off his slavery, but his face was always toward the dark pillar of hope now turning once again.

***⁎** When Coleridge left Bristol after his unsuccessful lecturing tour of 1813-14, a strong effort was made by Cottle, at Southey's suggestion, to induce him to return to Keswick. The Southey-Cottle correspondence of 1814 is interesting, as showing how ignorant of the facts of Coleridge's life it was possible for his friends to be. Cottle had newly learned that Coleridge was under the dominion of opium. Coleridge had then been an habitual opium-eater at least ten years. Southey believed that Coleridge had "sources of direct emolument open to him in *The Courier*, and in *The Eclectic Review*." "No advantage," says Cottle, "would arise from recording dialogues with Mr. Coleridge ; it is sufficient to state that Mr. C.'s repugnance to visit Greta Hall, and to apply his talents in the way suggested b Mr. Southey, was invincible." My strong conviction is that the chief bugbear for Coleridge at Greta Hall was none other than Southey himself.

CHAPTER X.

A FEW days before Coleridge settled at Highgate he
wrote a letter to Mr. Gillman, in which he detailed
with frankness the temptations to which his besetting
weakness exposed him of acting a deception which prior
habits of rigid truthfulness made it impossible for him to
speak. "I have full belief," he wrote, "that your
anxiety need not be extended beyond the first week, and
for the first week I shall not, I must not, be permitted to
leave the house, except with you. Delicately or indeli-
cately, this must be done, and both your servants and
the assistant must receive absolute commands from you."
A more resolute determination could not have been
made by a man whose will had never been sapped by
disease. We have no reason to doubt its sincerity, and
only the idlest gossip to question its faithful observance.
It is true that De Quincey said that Coleridge never
conquered his evil habit; true, too, that irresponsible
persons have alleged that down to his death Coleridge
continued to obtain supplies of laudanum surreptitiously
from a chemist in the Tottenham Court Road. But the
burden of proof is in favour of Mr. Gillman's clear assurance that the habit was eventually overcome.

In that first letter to Mr. Gillman, Coleridge stated in these terms the conditions on which he became an inmate of his house : " With respect to pecuniary remuneration, allow me to say, I must not at least be suffered to make any addition to your family expenses, though I cannot offer anything that would be in any way adequate to my sense of the service ; for that indeed there could not be a compensation, as it must be returned in kind by esteem and grateful affection." We have no good reason to fear that Coleridge ever ceased, during the eighteen years in which he remained under Mr. Gillman's roof, to regard his domesticity in the same light of pecuniary independence.

When he arrived at Highgate he brought with him the proof sheets of as much as was written of his " Christabel." The poem was published towards June of the same year, 1816, and met with a curious reception. Since its production in the years 1797 and 1800, it had enjoyed an extraordinary celebrity in manuscript among Coleridge's private friends. Almost every leading poet of the age had read it or heard it read. Two poets had given it a kind of public recognition. Byron had quoted from it, and Scott had adopted its metrical peculiarity, the substitution of accentual for syllabic scansion. Most of the leading critics were familiar with it. Hazlitt knew it intimately, and Leigh Hunt remembered it so well that in its printed form he was able to point out the omission of a line. Many copies had existed in manuscript, and Coleridge had been repeatedly importuned, at gatherings of literary people, to read it or recite from it. The verdict of his auditors on occasions when he yielded to the solicitation had, so far as he knew, been more than favourable ; it had been enthusiastic. Thus when Coleridge printed his poem, it was natural that he should look for a public reception from his friends corresponding, if not commensurate, with their private comments. In this he was grievously disappointed. Hardly a good word was said for " Christabel" by any leading review in 1816–17. *The Edinburgh Review* said that the poem was " the most notable piece of impertinence of which the press had lately been guilty," and " one of the boldest experiments " that had yet been tried on " the patience and understanding of the public." This review was written by Hazlitt, and *The Anti-Jacobin Review, Blackwood's Magazine*, and *The Examiner*, among others, were no less virulent in their censures. The public verdict seems to have been more favourable. At least two editions of the volume containing " Christabel" were published in the first year. The satisfactory evidences of sale may, however, have indicated no more than that public interest which is always excited in a book that is intemperately condemned.

Coleridge felt the material as well as the critical injury inflicted upon him. But less than the avowed enmity of his outspoken critics he felt the utter silence and detractive compliments of other writers. *The Quarterly Review*, of which Southey was the main support, did not notice " Christabel" even at the moment when its influential rivals were attacking the poem, and its author, with equal injury and injustice. Not wholly discouraged, and now once again actively at work, Coleridge published two Lay Sermons in 1816 and 1817, and in the latter year he

brought out his " Biographia Literaria." This book was
written mainly at Calne, in 1815, a period in which,
according to the letters of certain of his friends, he was
wholly given up to the sensual indulgence of opium, and
the idle talk that was supposed to pay for his board.   The
" Biographia Literaria " was, as its title indicates, designed
to be a record of his literary career.   It fulfils its avowed
function very indifferently.   A narrative more inconse-
quential was perhaps never put forth.   It is not a matter
for surprise that a mind like Coleridge's, having charged
itself with the task of narrating material incidents, should
find itself engrossed in such spiritual issues as arise out
of them.   And yet Coleridge had in a high degree the
faculty of direct and vigorous narrative.   The letters that
he wrote from Germany afford abundant evidence of his
art as a narrator, and indeed the " Biographia Literaria "
contains passages—such as the account of the canvassing
tour in the interests of *The Watchman*—which show that
Coleridge had nearly every natural quality of the story-
teller.   Nevertheless, the " Biographia Literaria " is inconclusive as a record of the author's literary life.   It
gives few facts, and omits many leading incidents.   Not
a word does it contain that relates to the important first
period at Bristol ; and of the journalistic career in London
it affords only a general account.   Instead of such matters
of fact, it gives exhaustive explanations of the workings
of the author's mind.   Naturally enough these explanations are often germane to the first business of the book,
as where the principles are expounded on which the
" Lyrical Ballads " were written.   Less proper to such a
work are certain philosophical expositions of the Hart-

leian theory, of Kant's and Fichte's writings, and sundry digressions on the nature of the imagination or plastic power. The book as a whole is, however, a thing of great price, and where it touches the principles of poetic composition it is hardly less than priceless. The chapters of just criticism and noble praise of Wordsworth were written at a time when Wordsworth held no real position as a poet. Such was Coleridge's insight and such his loyalty. An author's friends usually find it very easy to belaud him after the public has pronounced in his favour, but grievously difficult to their courage and loyalty to speak up for him while he is struggling his way to recognition. Coleridge, at least, found matters so. The reception of the "Biographia Literaria" on its publication in 1817 was as unfavourable as the reception of "Christabel" had been the year before. *Blackwood's Magazine* pronounced its opinions to be "wild ravings," and likened the vanity of the author to the deplorable deception of Joanna Southcote, who mistook a complaint in the bowels for the divine afflatus. The "grasp of Hazlitt's powerful hand" in *The Edinburgh Review*, which had previously "crumpled up the poet's verses like so much waste paper," was now put forth to reveal "the cant of Morality," which, like "the cant of Methodism," came to close the scene of Coleridge's literary life. "Our disappointed demagogue," said Hazlitt, "keeps up that 'pleasurable poetic fervour' which has been the cordial and bane of his existence, by indulging his maudlin egotism and his mawkish spleen in fulsome eulogies of his own virtues and nauseous abuse of his contemporaries, in making excuses for doing nothing himself, and assigning bad motives for what others have done." In 1817 Coleridge published his "Zapolya" also. This play was written, as we have seen, in 1815, though it seems probable that it was designed a year earlier. Coleridge appears to have hinted to Byron his desire to follow up his success with "Remorse," and Byron, still possessing influence at Drury Lane, gave him cordial encouragement. The play was rejected at the theatres for the reason assigned on an earlier page of this biography, and towards the end of 1817, about two years after its production, it was published as a Christmas tale. In form the dramatic poem was intended to imitate the "Winter's Tale" of Shakespeare, except that the subdivision into two parts, corresponding to the interval between the first and second acts, gave it the appearance of two plays on different periods of the same tale. The effect of the whole work was not, however, much disturbed by this subdivision, which, as Coleridge said, did not render the imagination less disposed to take up the required position. As a drama "Zapolya" was clearly deficient in qualities essential to success on the boards, even in days when "Remorse" and "Bertram" were not too undramatic to hold the stage. As a Christmas tale it proved popular at a time when such Yule-tide literature as the "Christmas Carol" was unknown. "Zapolya" sold to the extent of two thousand copies in six weeks, and Coleridge's earnings thereby would have been no less substantial than timely but for an accident that has yet to be recorded. The prolific year of 1817 witnessed yet another publication, a volume entitled "Sibylline Leaves." This was a collection of all Coleridge's poetical compositions from 1793 to the date of issue, with the addition of about twelve new poems, and with the exception of the dramatic writings, of "Christabel," and of the contents of the volume of 1796, whereof the copyright had been bought by Cottle. The collection had been made in 1815 at Calne, and was probably suggested by the circumstance that in that year Wordsworth had omitted Coleridge's four poems in reprinting his "Lyrical Ballads." In the same year the "Sibylline Leaves" was put into type by Longmans, but publication was delayed owing to vexatious causes, to which the author refers in a preface.

The book embodied the choicest of Coleridge's poetry. In addition to "The Ancient Mariner" and "Love," it contained "The Three Graves," a poem reprinted from *The Friend* of 1810. This poem, which was assigned by Coleridge to the period of his residence at Stowey, 1796–97, is quite the most interesting psychological study that he has given us. It was suggested by study of the Oba traditions, and by the curious superstitions of the Copper Indians, described by Samuel Hearne, a servant of the Hudson's Bay Company, in his account of a search for the copper rivers of North America. The book was probably read by Coleridge and Wordsworth together, for Wordsworth's poem, "The Forsaken Indian Woman," depicts with great fervour and picturesqueness a scene which Hearne describes in his plain homespun. What Coleridge borrowed from the rude sailor's narrative is even more important than Wordsworth's splendid appropriation. The intention was to show that the overwhelming power of an idea on health and life is not an effect to be seen in savage peoples only.

"Sibylline Leaves" was no more favourably received than "Christabel" had been. One of its critics, *Blackwood's Magazine,* said that the public accepted it as they would accept a "lying lottery puff, or a quack advertisement." It is hardly necessary to go farther in order to show that in 1817, after the production of nearly all his poetic work by which the world now sets store—"The Ancient Mariner," "Christabel," "Kubla Khan," "The Three Graves," "France, an Ode," "Fears in Solitude," "The Hymn before Sunrise in the Vale of Chamouni," "Frost at Midnight," and "Remorse"—Coleridge's acceptance at the hands of the professional guides to literature was hardly more than might have been due to a literary impostor and charlatan. We must realize this sure fact in all the fulness of its significance if we would rightly understand the disastrous effect of the world's neglect on Coleridge's later work, on his mind, and perhaps on his character and habits. Coleridge was deeply injured in pride and in purse, and though he did not proclaim his wrongs from the housetops, he made no effort to conceal them. In the torture of pride, of debased and material prospects marred, he probably made some unjust accusations of which he had afterwards to repent and which he had to retract. Scott found it necessary to protest that if he had appropriated from Coleridge a metrical peculiarity, if he had anticipated the author of "Christabel" with stories written in octosyllabics with anapæstic variations, he had penned no single line in his disparagement. Byron, too, was not slow to repeat a cordial eulogy whereof Coleridge had never had cause to question the sincerity. Still the poet suffered under the open assaults of declared enemies, and the hidden enmity of silent friends. If at this crisis of his hopes—the close of 1817—he doubted the friendship of Southey, shall we charge him with disloyalty in view of the fact that *The Quarterly Review* (by Coleridge's own statement) had not a word to say for " Christabel," for the " Biographia Literaria," " Zapolya," " Sibylline Leaves," and *The Friend ?* Let us not forget that Southey was the " chief support " of the review at that period, and, by his *own* account, a person of great influence with its editor. Then let us remember that this was no ordinary crisis in his brother-in-law's fortunes. The attacks of Coleridge's enemies were now as false and virulent as those of Southey's own enemies had been bitter, merciless, and injurious, four years earlier, when Coleridge spoke up unfalteringly for his friend. Even granting the best defence of Southey's silence, that he did not admire Coleridge and his work, and could not conscientiously champion either the one or other when assailed, there remains the yet more painful fact that malice had made free with Coleridge's personal character in a way that rendered it imperative on his brother-in-law to assure himself that he deserved his unpopularity or was cruelly injured by it.

Not content with denying to Coleridge any honourable place as a poet, the press affixed to what it called his " cant of morality," and " cant of Methodism," a distinct charge of corrupt life. There can be no sort of doubt as to what was meant by many innuendoes of hypocrisy ; it was clearly the common talk of the criticasters of the

period, and even of some writers who merit a less dis-
honouring name, that Coleridge was guilty in respect to
the wife of his host. The charge was shameful, and
worse than false. Though Coleridge lived more than
twenty years apart from his wife, the breath of scandal
did not touch him otherwise than in this regard. Men
like Stuart who had no desire to extol Coleridge's virtues,
and other witnesses quite as hostile, to whom a moral
dereliction could hardly be a mortal offence, were loud
in praise of the purity of his walk in life. Coleridge was
naturally a man of bounding animal spirits, but, as we
see in the records of Dr. Carlyon, his companion during
the German tour, his animal spirits were those of a
healthy boy. Even those suspicions of excess at the
time of enlistment which his family entertained and some
hostile critics have perpetuated, are seen to be groundless.
If Coleridge was at any period guilty of offence against the
moral law it must have been in those early days when, as
he says, he knew "just so much of folly" as "made
maturer years more wise." In later years his walk
became, more than ever, that of a man who had never so
much as a temptation to such offence. It is a curious
fact, which any careful reader of his letters may verify, that
when he became a slave to opium, his spiritual consciousness became more active, and his watchfulness of the
encroachments of the baser impulses of his nature more
keen. If his excesses in this regard were what Southey
described them, guilty animal indulgences, it is a strange
problem in psychology why the whole spiritual nature of
the man should undergo a manifest exaltation. Every
one who was brought into contact with Coleridge in the

darkest days of his subjection to opium, observed this extraordinary moral transfiguration. Cottle noticed it; Wordsworth described it in words that few of us who love Coleridge can read without tears; even Stuart in his dunderheaded way remarked that from 1808 to 1814 he never once heard Coleridge use a sentence that would have dishonoured "a clergyman." Southey did not observe this curious change, but that was because he saw next to nothing of Coleridge after January, 1804, except during a few months of 1806 and of 1810.

CHAPTER XI.

THE story of this broken life is all but told. Disappointed in his hopes as an author, depressed by his debts for board and lodgings, harassed by anxieties about his son who was now at Oxford,[1] conscious that the allowance made to his wife—the moiety of the Wedgewood pension—was barely sufficient for her needs, Coleridge's health and spirits flagged. Towards December, 1817, Wordsworth wrote to John Payne Collier to solicit his interest in a new course of lectures projected by Coleridge. "He is now far from well in body or spirits," Wordsworth writes, "the former is suffering from *various* causes, and the latter from depression." Charles Lamb warmly seconded Wordsworth's efforts on Coleridge's behalf. "He is in bad health," wrote Lamb, "and worse mind, and unless something is done to lighten his heart, he will soon be reduced to extremities; and even these," the inveterate punster added, "are not in

[1] His first son was sent up to the University in 1815, and at this, the darkest period of Coleridge's slavery to opium, Southey generously got together a subscription to defray the necessary expenses. When it became necessary to make provision for the residence of the younger son at Cambridge, Coleridge found himself equal to a father's duty in that regard.

the best condition." The result of the efforts put forth, partly by Collier, but mainly by Coleridge, was that a course of fourteen lectures was delivered in Fleur de Luce Court, Fetter Lane, in 1818, beginning the 27th of January and ending in March. Shakespeare was the subject of three of these lectures, and the remaining lectures of the course were devoted to a wide range of literature. Coleridge was not in his best condition, but the lectures were by much the most successful he ever delivered, both as to the number of his auditors and the extent of his earnings. He appears to have kept his engagements at this period as faithfully as in 1806, and in 1811–12.

It seems probable that his earnings from these lectures of 1818 were about one hundred and fifty pounds. Such a sum would have been of material service at this juncture but for an untoward circumstance already alluded to in general terms. This was the failure of his publishers early in 1819. The disaster was of vital consequence to Coleridge. It is difficult to realize what the precise relations may have been in which Coleridge stood to his publishers. The firm in question had published everything put forth by Coleridge later than "Christabel" in 1816, and that was published by Murray. Thus they held the "Biographia Literaria," "Sibylline Leaves," "Zapolya," and a remodelled edition of *The Friend*. If they bargained for the copyright, or, as seems probable, for the half-copyright, it is clear that they had not paid the price ; if they were responsible to the author for royalties, it is no less clear that an important sum was still due from them. The puzzling fact is the sequel.

In order to recover possession of his works Coleridge paid into the bankrupt estate the whole sum of his earnings from the lectures delivered in Fleur de Luce Court, and in addition to this payment he became chargeable with a debt of something like fifty pounds. Coleridge's letters on this subject are inconclusive ; only the recovery of original documents would make the circumstances clear. What is abundantly evident is that, after the rapid exaltation of his hopes, which came of the undoubted success of a strong effort, Coleridge was as suddenly cast back into pecuniary difficulties and the depression of soul that accompanied them. It was as though the Nemesis of disaster dogged his steps. Again and again he protested in his letters that whatever the measure of his responsibility for talents wasted, he had never been free from anxiety for his material welfare. He said no more than any impartial view of his life will prove to be true. In the darkest hour of his subjection to opium, in the lowest depths of what his friends knew by the name of indulgence, he worked as few men can work even under conditions the most favourable to their temperaments. The silly cuckoo-cry that Coleridge abandoned himself to idle dreams, and took single pounds in charity when he might have earned hundreds by vigorous effort, has come to us in part from the lips of a man who was so far from labouring under the long odds of physical health and monetary failure by which Coleridge's life was constantly hampered, that he could not do his daily work if a cock crew in the street, or if a dog barked in the next garden.

What little remains to be told of Coleridge's life is as

sad a story of noble labour spurned, and of mighty talents
underprized, as the annals of literature contains.   It is a
story of work without honour, and work without hope.
Embarrassed by many immediate debts, to which it was
now no longer possible that debts incurred for opium
could contribute, Coleridge returned to the hack labours
that had already eaten up the prime years of his manhood.   To pay board and lodgings, and to do some
little for his son Hartley, at Oxford, Coleridge engaged
himself, " to obtain an honourable sufficiency, by writing
school books."   Not even with this was the cup of
his humiliation full ; but one thinks it must have
run over and down the sides when, a little later, it
became necessary to " write sermons for lazy clergymen,"
who stipulated that the composition should be " more
than respectable."   The " dark pillar " of hope had
turned and turned again, and Coleridge, the most " wonderful " man ever known to Wordsworth, the only person
that answered to Hazlitt's idea of a man of genius, the
largest and most spacious intellect that De Quincey had
yet found among men ; Coleridge, the dreamer of great
dreams, was toiling at fifty years of age each day and
hour of his writing power, to pay some two pounds ten
shillings a week for board and lodgings.   The Gillmans
were attached to him by every tie of esteem and love,
and the day must have been dark for them in which they
could have beclouded Coleridge's life with one thought
of his pecuniary indebtedness ; but none the less, but all
the more, for the affection that would not exact its material dues, Coleridge—if he was a truthful man—felt in
honour bound to discharge them.   In January, 1821, he

writes that he is working five to six hours a day ; and in December, 1822, he writes that he is working every day and nearly every hour of waking time. Like humbler slaves of the pen, Coleridge had no thought of quarrelling with his bread and butter. He knew, with a pang only too poignant, that *Blackwood's Magazine* had laughed at his "Christabel," and ridiculed those "wild ravings" of the "Biographia Literaria," which it likened to the deplorable delusion of the woman who had the pain in her stomach ; he knew that the same authority had told the world that the volume containing "The Ancient Mariner," and "The Three Graves," was being received like a "lying lottery puff, or a quack advertisement." Nevertheless, he was compelled, in 1821, to go to *Blackwood* with his hat in his hand, and ask to be allowed to write little articles for little pay, just as he had gone to *The Courier* ten years before, and prayed to be allowed to condense reports from the other newspapers for a wage that he did not dare to stipulate.

But Coleridge's material condition was not worse than his intellectual prospect. To write schoolbooks for "an honourable sufficiency," and sermons for a bare pittance that was perhaps something less than honourable, was a bad business in itself; but it threatened consequences that were more to be feared than its own immediate abasement. The sense of extinguished power was growing upon Coleridge daily amid this humiliating toil. Life was slipping away, and though the number and extent of his published works showed that he had not been idle in his generation, the works that had been wholly or mainly carried to their completion bore only a small proportion to those that he had designed. The grain he had housed was harvest enough for a smaller man, but Coleridge was a giant, and more than half of all that he had meant to carry still lay on the field. " From circumstances," he writes in January, 1821, " the *main* portion of my harvest is still on the ground, ripe indeed, and only waiting, a few for the sickle, but a large part only for the *sheaving*, and carting, and housing ; but from all this I must turn away, must let them rot as they lie, and be as though they had never been, for I must go and gather blackberries and earth-nuts, or pick mushrooms and gild oak-apples for the palates and fancies of chance customers." The lack of opportunity was much, but the lack of wonted power was more. Such agony as came of the consciousness of extinguished vigour was not easy to express ; but Coleridge has expressed it in words as pathetic and beautiful, perhaps, as ever came from any man :—

> " All Nature seems at work.   Slugs leave their lare—
> The bees are stirring—birds are on the wing—
> And Winter, slumbering in the open air,
> Wears on his smiling face a dream of Spring !
> And I, the while, the sole unbusy thing,
> Nor honey make, nor pair, nor build, nor sing.
>
> Yet well I ken the banks where amaranths blow,
> Have traced the fount whence streams of nectar flow.
> Bloom, O ye amaranths ! bloom for whom ye may,
> For me ye bloom not !   Glide, rich streams, away !
> With lips unbrightened, wreathless brow, I stroll ;
> And would you learn the spells that drowse my soul ?
> WORK WITHOUT HOPE draws nectar in a sieve,
> And HOPE without an object cannot live."

In 1820 Coleridge had his sons with him at Highgate, and two years later his daughter visited him. Hartley, after an Oxford career that terminated unfortunately, was then poetizing a little and thinking about keeping school at Ambleside. Sara had just published her first book. In 1825 Coleridge read before the Royal Society of Literature an essay on "The Prometheus of Æschylus," and in the same year he published his philosophical work entitled, "Aids to Reflection." The production of this book had a good effect on his spirits; its reception was more than favourable; the tide of Coleridge's fame had at length begun to flow. In this year, 1825, Coleridge received a pension of a hundred guineas from the private purse of the king, George IV. For accepting this timely help in his hour of need, he was called a "Tory pensioner," "a puffed-up partizan," and the public was told that "trampling on the labouring classes" was "the religion at the bottom of his heart, for the simple reason that he was himself supported out of that last resource of the enemies of the people, the Pension List." The "last resource of the enemies of the people" failed Coleridge, however, in his hour of still greater need. In 1830 the king died, and the pension stopped. Coleridge, thinking he had a claim, appealed to Lord Grey, who offered him a sum equal to two years' pension; but these temporizing terms the poet declined. He then wrote to Brougham, who in the old days had professed to admire him as a journalist, but Brougham appears to have done nothing. Thus, on the verge of sixty, Coleridge was once again entirely without calculable resources. He wrote a little for *Blackwood*, and continued to earn small sums by various labours equivalent in usefulness and dignity to the aforesaid gilding of oak-apples.

From 1820 onwards the house of Mr. Gillman had gradually acquired a unique distinction as a rallying-point for intellectual activity. The residence of Coleridge with the Gillmans drew to Highgate many men and women who were celebrated in their several walks. One day a week or oftener there gathered about Coleridge a select band of young men who looked up to him as to a master. Among them were Edward Irving, Frederick Denison Maurice, Arthur H. Hallam, Joseph Henry Green, Julius Hare, and Coleridge's nephew, H. N. Coleridge. Men of an older generation often joined this weekly gathering, and of these there were Basil Montagu, whose estrangement from Coleridge in 1811 did not forbid a genial social intercourse.[1] Charles Lamb was often of the circle, and, on the rare occasions of their visits to London, Wordsworth and John Wilson were at Highgate. It does not appear that Shelley ever met Coleridge at Mr. Gillman's or elsewhere, and this was probably due, not to any lack of appreciation on Shelley's part—he described him as "a hooded eagle among blinking owls"—but to the circumstance that Shelley's circle among poets was that of Leigh Hunt ; and after 1817 the editor of *The Examiner* could hardly

[1] My conjecture would be that the estrangement from Basil Montagu (involving in the course of years a still deeper cause of grievance), must lie at the basis of any satisfactory explanation of the first part of the mysterious letter (from Coleridge to Allsop, dated Ramsgate, Oct. 8, 1822), which has been a puzzle to all biographers. My further inference is, that the second part of the Ramsgate letter has references to the writer's sons, Hartley and Derwent.

be a welcome guest or sincere disciple where Coleridge was practically in the position of the honoured host and prophet. It is conceivable that the same cause operated to keep Keats from the weekly gatherings ; but walking one day, towards 1818, in a lane near Highgate, Coleridge met "a loose, slack, not well-dressed youth." It was Keats. "Let me carry away the memory, Coleridge, of having pressed your hand," he said. It was Keats indeed : I can think of no other man who could have said just that. Rather later than this he said, "I can humble myself to nothing . . . but the memory of great men." Keats's occasional utterances are hardly to be matched in depth of human feeling. At this time, 1818, *Blackwood's Magazine* was styling him "Johnny Keats." "He was as little like 'Johnny Keats,'" said his brother, "as the Holy Ghost."

Among those who were constant, if not prominent, at the gatherings of Coleridge's disciples was a young man named Thomas Allsop. Coleridge met this extraordinary friend during the lectures of 1818, when he introduced himself to the lecturer by a letter left at the door of the hall in Fleur de Luce Court. It is abundantly clear that Coleridge cultivated the friendship, though it is hard to realize that there can have been a strong intellectual bond. A sufficient idea of the gentleman's mental equipment will be obtained from the fact that, finding his propriety disturbed by the couplet in "Christabel"—

> "Sir Leoline, the baron rich,
> Hath a toothless mastiff bitch,"

Mr. Allsop suggested to the poet this delicate and euphonious emendation—

> "Sir Leoline, the baron round,
> Had a toothless mastiff hound."

He tells us that Coleridge for some reason did not adopt the change. If any reader should still be curious to estimate the intellectual calibre of this last of the friends that Coleridge annexed in a pilgrimage that brought many strange companions, let him read this graphic account of Charles Lamb and his "double." "I never knew any one who at all approached or resembled our delightful housemate (Lamb). I am wrong; I once met a man with his smile,—HIS SMILE. There is nothing like it upon earth ; unless, perchance, this man survives. . . . He was, I believe, a stockbroker, and had been with his son to traverse the haunts of his childhood, near Lymington ; *with his son*, afflicted with a sudden and complete deafness ; hence, perchance, these sweet smiles springing from, and compounded of, love and pain. Yet this man had never known Lamb ; still his smile was the same. . . . To those who wish to see the only thing left on earth, *if it is still left*, of Lamb, his best and most beautiful remain,—his smile, I indicate its possessor—Mr. Harman, of Throgmorton Street." To grasp the full significance of this beautiful "situation," it is only necessary to imagine a lover of Lamb traversing Throgmorton Street in search of a stockbroker named Mr. Harman, and then waiting, or "perchance" asking, for his—smile. It is not an inference that dishonours Mr. Allsop to say that his friendship with Coleridge had probably a basis of material benefits conferred and received. Whatever the bond that knit together two such men, it is a fact that Coleridge wrote to Allsop a series of important letters. These letters Allsop published in due course, apparently to the discomfiture of Southey and a few other friends, and certainly at the cost of his personal peace.

Coleridge's attractions as a talker were great, as we have seen, in the days of the "Salutation and Cat," of the canvass in the interests of *The Watchman*, and of the German tour ; but in the days at Highgate they were probably at their best. The only satisfying record of Coleridge's powers in conversation is the volume of "Table Talk," collected by H. N. Coleridge, from the end of 1822 to the middle of July, 1834. This book carries the sure proof of education that is almost without parallel, and of reading, thought, and observation, that outstrides, I think, the intellectual equipment of every Englishman since Bacon. But here we have the essence of what Coleridge said, and to other records we must turn for accounts of how he said it. We shall take two witnesses only, and they shall be sufficiently unlike. First, T. N. Talfourd :—

" He has yet completed no adequate memorials of his genius, yet it is most unjust to assert that he has done little or nothing. To refute this assertion, there are his ' Wallenstein ;' his love poems of intensest beauty ; his ' Ancient Mariner,' with its touches of profoundest tenderness amidst the wildest and most bewildering terrors ; his holy and sweet tale of ' Christabel,' with its rich enchantments and richer humanities; the depths, the sublimities, and the pensive sweetness of his ' Tragedy;' the heart-dilating sentiments scattered through his ' Friend'; and the stately imagery which breaks upon us at every turn of the golden paths of his metaphysical labyrinths. And if he had a power within him mightier than that which even these glorious creations indicate, shall he be censured because he has deviated from the ordinary course of the age in its development, and instead of committing his imaginative wisdom to the press has delivered it from his living lips? He has gone about in the true spirit of an old Greek bard, with a noble carelessness of self, giving fit utterance to the Divine spirit within him. Who that has ever heard can forget him? his mild benignity, the unbounded variety of his knowledge, the fast-succeeding products of his imagination, the child-like simplicity with which he rises from the driest and commonest theme into the wildest magnificence of thought, pouring on the soul a stream of beauty and of wisdom to mellow and enrich it for ever? The seeds of poetry, the materials for thinking, which he has thus scattered will not perish. The records of his fame are not in books only, but on the fleshly tablets of young hearts, who will not suffer it to die even in the general ear, however base and unfeeling criticism may deride their gratitude."

Our second witness shall be Carlyle. This is the famous description in " The Life of Sterling : "—

" The good man—he was now getting old, towards

sixty perhaps, and gave you the idea of a life that had
been full of sufferings ; a life heavy-laden, half-vanquished,
still swimming painfully in seas of manifold physical and
other bewilderment.   Brow and head were round and of
massive weight, but the face was flabby and irresolute.
The deep eyes, of a light hazel, were as full of sorrow as
of inspiration ; confused pain looked mildly from them,
as in a kind of mild astonishment.   The whole figure
and air, good and amiable otherwise, might be called
flabby and irresolute ; expressive of weakness under
possibility of strength.   He hung loosely on his limbs,
with knees bent, and stooping attitude ; in walking he
rather shuffled than decisively stept ; and a lady once
remarked he never could fix which side of the garden-
walk would suit him best, but continually shifted, cork-
screw fashion, and kept trying both ; a heavy-laden, high-
aspiring, and surely much-suffering man.   His voice,
naturally soft and good, had contracted itself into a
plaintive snuffle and sing-song ; he spoke as if preaching
—you could have said preaching earnestly and almost
hopelessly the weightiest things.   I still recollect his
‘ object ’ and ‘ subject,’ terms of continual recurrence in
the Kantean province ; and how he sang and snuffled
them into ‘ om-m-ject ’ and ‘ sum-m-mject,’ with a kind of
solemn shake or quaver as he rolled along.   No talk in
his century or in any other could be more surprising.”

In the summer of 1828 Coleridge made a tour into
Flanders with Wordsworth and his daughter Dora.   On
his return he brought out a collected edition of his
poetical works.   Late in 1829 Coleridge’s daughter Sara

married her cousin, Henry Nelson Coleridge, and removed from Keswick to Hampstead, taking her mother with her. Thus Coleridge and his wife were near neighbours during the last years of his life, but it is not stated that they ever met again. After living apart for nineteen years it was hardly likely that they could ever come together on terms of amity, or meet on terms equivalent to armed neutrality.

Coleridge continued to work amid many indications of breaking health. His constant assurance that he possessed a vast harvest ready for the sheaving did not prove to be fallacious. Four large volumes were but a part of the work which he had been doing in the dark throughout many silent years. In 1831 his health continued to fail. A year later Wordsworth wrote that Coleridge and his sister Dorothy were "going, *pari passu*, along the path of sickness, towards a blessed immortality." In that year Coleridge printed the last part of his beautiful "Youth and Age"—

> " Dew-drops are the gems of morning, ...
> But the tears of mournful eve !
> Where no hope is, life's a warning
> That only serves to make us grieve, ...
> When we are old ;
> That only serves to make us grieve
> With oft and tedious taking-leave,
> Like some poor nigh-related guest, . . —
> That may not rudely be dismisst ;
> Yet hath outstay'd his welcome while, ...
> And tells the jest without the smile.". .

This great man was dying with the clear consciousness

that the world denied him his due. Long ago life had
lost its charm of hope for him, and where no hope was,
life was no better than the stern lamp of a ship that lights
only the path that is past. The time had been when he had
fretted under the sense of work without hope, and talents
that he was compelled to waste. But that time was now
gone by. The fiery column that rose before his youth
was the dark pillar that stood behind his age. He was
reconciled to his dismissal; he had told the jest without
the smile. Towards the end of 1833 he wrote his
epitaph—

> " Stop, Christian passer-by :—Stop, child of God
> And read, with gentle breast.   Beneath this sod
> A poet lies, or that which once seemed he—
> O, lift one thought in prayer for S. T. C. —
> That he who many a year with toil of breath
> Found death in life may here find life in death !
> Mercy for praise,—to be forgiven for fame,—
> He asked, and hoped, through Christ.   Do thou the same."

Towards the end he grew anxious as to not having
seen much of Charles Lamb latterly, and he wrote a
touching letter hinting at his faults as a friend. But
Lamb had never ceased to love him. "Not an unkind
thought has passed in my brain about you," Lamb
writes; "if ever you thought an offence, much less wrote
it against me, it must have been in the times of Noah,
and the great waters swept it away. Mary's most kind
love, . . . here she is crying for mere love over your
letter." The beautiful friendship was to end as it had
begun. Early in 1834, Coleridge, in memory of the days
of that visit of the "gentle Charles" to Stowey in 1797,

wrote these words under the poem beginning, "This Lime-tree Bower my Prison:" "Charles and Mary Lamb, dear to my heart, yea, as it were *my heart.*" In a copy of Beaumont and Fletcher he wrote—

"*Midnight.*

"God bless you, dear Charles Lamb ; I am dying : I feel I have not many weeks left.

"Mr. Gillman's, Highgate."

Death came suddenly to Coleridge as to every man. No matter how long it may be waited for, when it comes it comes as a surprise. He died on Friday, the 25th of July, 1834.

Coleridge's son-in-law sent the tidings to Wordsworth in Westmoreland, and when the old poet read the news aloud to his family his voice faltered and broke. "He has long been dead to me," said Southey, " but his decease has naturally wakened up old recollections." "Coleridge is dead," Lamb muttered to himself continually. " Coleridge is dead, Coleridge is dead ! " To the woman who had nursed his friend, Lamb gave five guineas when he went to Highgate for the first time after the funeral. "His great and dear spirit haunts me," Lamb wrote a little later. " He was my fifty-year-old friend without a dissension. Never saw I his likeness, nor probably the world can see it again." Lamb himself died before the end of the year.

They buried Coleridge in Highgate churchyard, and now under the crypt of the new school chapel—

> " The rapt one of the godlike forehead,
> The heaven-eyed creature sleeps in earth."

The grave had hardly closed on him when the world echoed with his praise. " Coleridge," said *Blackwood* (1834) " alone perhaps of all men that ever lived was always a poet—in all his moods, and they were many, inspired."

THE END.

BIBLIOGRAPHY.

BY

JOHN P. ANDERSON

(British Museum).

I. WORKS.

The Complete Works of S. T. Coleridge. With an introductory essay upon his philosophical and theological opinions. Edited by Professor Shedd. In seven volumes. New York, 1853, 8vo.
A re-issue of this edition was published at New York in 1884.

The Works of S. T. C. Prose and Verse. Complete, etc. Philadelphia [1884 ?], 8vo.

II. SMALLER COLLECTIONS.

The Poetical and Dramatic Works of S. T. C., with numerous additional poems, now first collected, and revised by the author. 3 vols. London, 1828, 8vo.
[A re-issue of this edition appeared in 1829.

The Poetical Works of S. T. C. 3 vols. London, 1834, 12mo.

The Poetical and Dramatic Works of S. T. C. With a life of the author. London, 1836, 12mo.

——Another Edition. With a memoir. [Edited by Sara and D. Coleridge]. 3 vols. Boston [U.S.], 1854, 8vo.

——Another Edition. Founded on the author's latest edition of 1834, with many additional pieces now first included, and with a collection of various readings. [Edited by R. H. Shepherd.] 4 vols. London, 1877, 8vo.

[Another Edition.] Poetical and Dramatic Works. 4 vols. London, 1880, 8vo.
This is a re-issue of the preceding, published by Macmillan, with supplement to vol. ii.

The Literary Remains of S. T. C., collected and edited by H. N. Coleridge. 4 vols. London, 1836-39, 8vo.

I. On the constitution of the Church and State, according to the idea of each. (Third edition.) II. Lay Sermons. (Second edition.) Edited from the author's corrected copies, with notes by H. N. Coleridge, London, 1839, 8vo.

Aids to Reflection and the Confessions of an Inquiring Spirit. By S. T. C. To which are added his Essays on Faith and the Book of Common Prayer. New edition, revised. [With the "preliminary essay" by J. Marsh.] (*Bohn's Standard Library.*) London, 1884, 8vo.

Table-Talk [edited by H. N. C., *i.e.*, Henry Nelson Coleridge] ... and the Rime of the Ancient Mariner, Christabel, etc. (*Morley's Universal Library.*) London, 1884, 8vo.

Miscellanies, æsthetic and literary: to which is added the Theory of Life ... Collected and arranged by T. Ashe. (*Bohn's Standard Library.*) London, 1885, 8vo.

III. POEMS.

The Poetical Works of Coleridge, Shelley, and Keats. Complete in one vol. 3 parts. Paris, 1829, 8vo.

The Poems of S. T. C. London, 1844, 8vo.

The Poems of S. T. C. London, 1848, 8vo.

The Poetical Works of T. Campbell and S. T. C. Edinburgh [1859], 8vo.

The Poems of S. T. C. Edited by D. and S. Coleridge. London, 1852, 12mo.

——Another Edition. London, 1857, 18mo.

The Poems of S. T. C. Edited by D. and S. Coleridge, with a biographical memoir by F. Freiligrath. [*Tauchnitz edition,* vol. 512.] Leipzig, 1860, 16mo.

The Poems of S. T. C. London, 1862, 16mo.

One of "Bell and Daldy's Pocket Volumes."

[Another copy.] London, 1864, 8vo.

A duplicate of the preceding with a new titlepage. Part of "Bell and Daldy's Elzevir Series of Standard Authors."

The Poems of S. T. C. Edited by Derwent and Sara Coleridge. With an appendix. A new edition. London, 1863, 8vo.

The Poetical Works of S. T. C. Edited, with a critical memoir, by W. M. Rossetti. Illustrated by T. Seccombe. London [1872], 8vo.

The Poetical Works of S. T. C. Edited, with an introductory memoir and illustrations, by W. B. Scott. London, [1874], 8vo.

The Poetical Works of S. T. C. London, [1878], 8vo.

The Poetical Works of Coleridge and Keats; with a memoir of each. 2 vols. New York, 1878, 8vo.

Part of a series of "British Poets. Riverside edition."

The Poetical Works of S. T. C. Edited, with an introductory memoir, by W. B. Scott. London [1880], 8vo.
Part of the "Excelsior Series."

The Poetical Works of S. T. C. Edited, with a critical memoir, by W. M. Rossetti, etc. [*Moxon's Popular Poets.*] London [1880], 8vo.

The Poetical Works of S. T. C. With Life, etc. Edinburgh, London [1881], 8vo.
Part of "The Landscape Series of Poets."

The Poems of S. T. C. With a prefatory notice . . . by J. Skipsey. London, 1884, 16mo.
One of a series, entitled "The Canterbury Poets."

The Poetical Works of S. T. C. Edited, with introduction and notes, by T. Ashe. (*Aldine edition of the British Poets.*) 2 vols. London, 1885, 8vo.

Poems on various subjects. London, 1796, 12mo.
Contains three or four sonnets by Charles Lamb.

——Second edition. To which are now added Poems by C. Lamb and C. Lloyd. Bristol, 1797, 12mo.

Poems. London [1800 ?], 8vo.

——Third edition. London, 1803, 12mo.

Lyrical Ballads, etc. [By Coleridge and Wordsworth.] London, 1798, 8vo.
Includes "The Ancient Mariner," "The Foster-Mother's Tale," "The Nightingale," and "The Dungeon."

——Second Edition. By William Wordsworth. 2 vols. London, 1800, 8vo.
Includes the same poems by Coleridge as in the preceding, with the addition of the poem on "Love."

Lyrical Ballads, etc. Third Edition. By William Wordsworth. 2 vols. London, 1802, 8vo.
Includes the same poems by Coleridge as in the Second Edition, with the exception of "The Dungeon," which is omitted.

Select Poetical Works, etc. London, 1852, 12mo.

Christabel, and the lyrical and imaginative Poems of S. T. C. Arranged and introduced by A. C. Swinburne. London, 1869, 16mo.
Part of "The Bayard Series."

Favorite Poems. Boston [U.S.], 1877, 16mo.

Fears in Solitude, written in 1798, during the alarm of an invasion. To which are added, France, an ode ; and Frost at Midnight. London, 1798, 4to.

Christabel ; Kubla Khan, a vision; The Pains of Sleep. London, 1816, 8vo.

——Second Edition. London, 1816, 8vo.

Ode on the departing year. Bristol, 1796, 4to.

Prospect of Peace. London, 1796, 4to.
Mentioned in Watt's "Bib. Brit." and in Lowndes; but there is no copy known.

The Raven, a Christmas tale.— Illustrated in eight plates. By an old Traveller. London, [1848 ?], obl. 4to.

The Rime of the Ancient Mariner. Illustrated by twenty-five poetic and dramatic scenes, designed and etched by D. Scott. Edinburgh, 1837, fol.

The Ancient Mariner, and other poems. London, 1844, 16mo.
Part of "Clarke's Cabinet Series."

The Rime of the Ancient Mariner. Illustrated [by E. H. Wehnert, B. Foster, and others]. London, 1857, 8vo.

The Ancient Mariner, etc. London, 1858, 32mo.
Part of the "Miniature Classical Library."

Coleridge's Ancient Mariner, and other poems. London, 1872, 8vo.
Part of "Chambers's English Classics," etc.

The Rime of the Ancient Mariner. Illustrated. London, [1875], 8vo.
Part of "The Choice Series."

Another edition. Illustrated by Doré. London, 1876, fol.

Another edition. Illustrated. Boston [U.S.], 1876, 24mo.
Part of the "Vest-Pocket series of standard and popular authors."

The Rime of the Ancient Mariner. (*Annotated Poems of English Authors. Edited by E. T. Stevens and D. Morris.*) London, 1878, 16mo.

Another edition. Illustrated by D. Scott, etc. London, 1883, 16mo.

The Ancient Mariner, Christabel, and Miscellaneous Poems. (*Ward & Lock's Popular Library of Literary Treasures.*) London, 1886, 8vo.

Sibylline Leaves. A collection of poems. (The whole, with the exception of a few from 1796, of the author's poetical compositions from 1793 to the present date.) London, 1817, 8vo.

The Devil's Walk : a poem by S. T. C. and R. Southey [or rather by Southey, with a few stanzas added by Coleridge]. Edited, with a biographical memoir (of Professor Porson) and notes, by H. W. Montagu. Second edition. (*Facetiæ, etc. Illustrated by Robert Cruikshank, vol.* ii.) London, 1831, 12mo.

——Ten Etchings illustrative of the Devil's Walk [a poem by R. Southey and S. T. C.] London, 1831, fol.

IV. DRAMATIC WORKS.

The Dramatic Works of S. T. C. Edited by Derwent Coleridge. A new edition. London, 1852, 8vo.

The Fall of Robespierre. An historic drama [in three acts and in verse. The first act by S. T. C., the second and third by R. Southey]. Cambridge, 1794, 8vo.

Osorio, a tragedy, as originally written in 1797, now first printed from a copy recently discovered . . . with the variorum readings of "Remorse," and a monograph on the history of the play in its earlier and later form, by the author of "Tennysoniana" [R. H. S., *i.e.*, R. H. Shepherd]. London, 1873, 8vo.

Remorse ; a tragedy in five acts [and in verse]. London, 1813, 8vo.
The two following editions of Remorse differ considerably from the above.

——Second edition. London, 1813, 8vo.

——Third edition. London, 1813, 8vo.

Zapolya : A Christmas Tale, in two parts : The prelude entitled "The Usurper's Fortune ;" and the sequel entitled "The Usurper's Fate." London, 1817, 8vo.

V. LETTERS.

Letters, conversations, and recollections of S. T. C., Edited by T. Allsop. 2 vols. London, 1836, 12mo.
——Second edition. [With a preface by R. A., *i.e.*, Robert Allsop?] London, 1858, 8vo.
——Third edition. London, 1864, 8vo.
A duplicate of the second edition, with a new titlepage and preface.
Unpublished Letters from S. T. C. to the Rev. John Prior Estlin. Communicated by Henry A. Bright. (*Philobiblon Society.*) [London, 1884], 4to.

VI. MISCELLANEOUS WORKS.

Aids to Reflection in the formation of a manly character on the several grounds of prudence, morality, and religion : illustrated by select passages from our elder divines, especially from Archbishop Leighton. London, 1825, 8vo.
——[Another edition.] Aids to Reflection. London, 1836, 8vo.
——Another edition. With a preliminary essay by J. Marsh. From the fourth London edition, with the author's last corrections, edited by H. N. Coleridge. Burlington [U.S.], 1840, 8vo.
—— Fifth edition, enlarged. Edited by H. N. Coleridge. 2 vols. London, 1843, 8vo.
——Sixth edition, enlarged. 2 vols. London, 1848, 16mo.
——Seventh edition (with several notes by the author). Edited by D. Coleridge. London, 1854, 8vo.

Aids to Reflection. — Another edition. London, 1861, 12mo.
——New edition, revised. With index and translations of the Greek and Latin quotations by T. Fenby. Liverpool, 1873, 8vo.
——Another edition. London, 1883, 12mo.
——Another edition. London, 1884, 12mo.
Biographia Literaria ; or, Biographical sketches of my literary life and opinions. By S. T. C. 2 vols. London, 1817, 8vo.
——Second edition, prepared in part by H. N. Coleridge, completed by his widow (Sara Coleridge). 2 vols. London, 1847, 16mo.
——New edition. From the second London edition, etc. 2 vols. New York, 1848, 12mo.
——Another edition. London, 1866, 12mo.
Blessed are ye that sow beside all waters. A lay sermon, addressed to the higher and middle classes, on the existing distresses and discontents. London, 1817, 8vo.
Conciones ad Populum ; or, Addresses to the People. Bristol, 1795, 8vo.
Confessions of an Inquiring Spirit. By S. T. C. Edited from the author's MS. by H. N. Coleridge. London, 1840, 8vo.
——Another edition. Confessions of an Inquiring Spirit, and some miscellaneous pieces. Edited from the author's MS. by H. N. Coleridge. [With an introduction by J. H. Green.] London, 1849, 16mo.
——Third edition. London, 1853, 12mo.
——Fourth edition. London, 1863, 12mo.

The Friend. A series of essays. London, 1812, 8vo.

> This work was published in 27 nos. from June 1, 1809, to March 15, 1810, and originally entitled, "The Friend; a literary, moral, and political weekly paper." It was mainly written by Coleridge.

——New edition. 3 vols. London, 1818, 8vo.

——Third edition, with the author's last corrections, and an appendix, etc. [Edited] by H. N. Coleridge. 3 vols. London, 1837, 12mo.

——Fourth edition. 3 vols. London, 1844, 12mo.

——Another edition. London, 1850, 12mo.

New edition, revised [by D. Coleridge]. 2 vols. London, 1863, 8vo.

——Another edition. [*Bohn's Standard Library.*] London, 1866, 8vo.

Essays on his own times; forming a second series of "The Friend." By S. T. C. Edited by his daughter (Sara Coleridge). 3 vols. London, 1850, 8vo.

> Consists mainly of S. T. C.'s contributions to the newspapers.

General Introduction to the Encyclopædia Metropolitana; or, A preliminary treatise on Method. London, 1845, 4to.

Treatise on Method, reprinted from the Encyclopædia Metropolitana. London, 1849, 8vo.

> Same work as the preceding. The essay itself is dated "January 1818."

A Hebrew Dirge, by H. Hurwitz, on the funeral of the Princess Charlotte, with a translation in English verse, by S. T. C. London, 1817, 8vo.

Hints towards the formation of a more comprehensive theory of Life. Edited by S. B. Watson. London, 1848, 12mo.

Lay Sermons, edited with the author's last corrections and notes, by D. Coleridge. Third edition. London, 1852, 8vo.

Lectures and notes on Shakspere and other English Poets. Now first collected, by T. Ashe. (*Bohn's Standard Library.*) London, 1883, 8vo.

The Life of Wesley; and rise and progress of Methodism. Third edition; by Robert Southey; with notes, by S. T. C., etc. 2 vols. London, 1846, 8vo.

——New edition; with notes by S. T. C., etc. 2 vols. London, 1858, 8vo.

Lives of Northern Worthies; by Hartley Coleridge, edited by his brother (Derwent Coleridge). A new edition, with the corrections of the author, and the marginal observations of S. T. C. 3 vols. London, 1852, 8vo.

A moral and political lecture [on the principles of freedom] delivered at Bristol. Bristol, [1795], 8vo.

> This is in substance the same as the first of the *Conciones.*

Notes and Lectures upon Shakespeare and some of the old Poets and Dramatists; with other Literary Remains. Edited by Mrs. H. N. Coleridge. 2 vols. London, 1849, 16mo.

> This work, the *Notes on English Divines,* and *Notes, theological, etc.,* are substantially reprints of the four vols. of "Literary Remains."

Notes on English Divines. Edited by the Rev. D. Coleridge. 2 vols. London, 1853, 8vo.

Notes on Stillingfleet [written in a copy of his "Origines Sacræ"], by S. T. C. [Edited by R. Garnett. Reprinted from The Athenæum.] Glasgow, 1875, 8vo.

Printed for private circulation.

Notes, theological, political, and miscellaneous. Edited by Derwent Coleridge. London, 1853, 8vo.

Omniana; or Horae Otiosiores. [By R. Southey and S. T. C.] London, 1812, 12mo.

On the Constitution of the Church and State, according to the idea of each : with aids towards a right judgment on the late Catholic Bill. London, 1830, 8vo.

——Fourth edition. Edited, with notes, by H. N. Coleridge. London, 1852, 8vo.

The Plot Discovered ; or an address to the people against ministerial treason. Bristol, 1795, 8vo.

Prospectus of a course of Lectures. By S. T. C. [London, 1818], 4to.

Seven Lectures on Shakespeare and Milton. . . . A List of all the MS. emendations in Mr. Collier's folio, 1632 ; and an introductory preface by J. P. Collier. London, 1856, 8vo.

There is a copy in the Library of the British Museum, with numerous newspaper cuttings and other extracts inserted.

Specimens of the Table Talk of . . . S. T. C. [Edited by H. N. C., *i.e.*, Henry Nelson Coleridge.] 2 vols. London, 1835, 12mo.

——Third edition. London, 1851, 8vo.

Specimens of the Table Talk of . . S. T. C. Another edition. London, [1874] 8vo.

Part of "Routledge's Standard Series."

The Table Talk [reprinted from the second edition of H. N. Coleridge's "Specimens"] and Omniana of S. T. C. With additional Table Talk from Allsop's "Recollections," and manuscript matter not before printed. Arranged and edited by T. Ashe. (*Bohn's Standard Library.*) London, 1884, 8vo.

The Statesman's Manual ; or the Bible the best guide to political skill and foresight; a lay-sermon [on Psal. lxxviii. 5-7]. With an appendix, containing comments and essays connected with the study of the inspired writings, London, 1816, 8vo.

The Temple ; sacred poems and private ejaculations, by George Herbert. [With notes by S. T. C.] London, 1857, 8vo.

The Piccolomini, or the first part of Wallenstein ; a drama, etc., by J. C. F. Von Schiller. Translated by S. T. C. London, 1800, 8vo.

The Death of Wallenstein, a tragedy in five acts. Translated by S. T. C. London, 1800, 8vo.

The Works of F. Schiller. The Piccolomini.—Death of Wallenstein. Translated by S. T. C. Vol. ii. (*Bohn's Standard Library.*) London, 1846, etc., 8vo.

Schiller's Tragedies: The Piccolomini ; and the Death of Wallenstein. Translated from

I I

the German by S. T. C. (*The Universal Library. Poetry, vol.* i.) London, 1853, etc., 8vo.

The Tragedies of Schiller. The Piccolomini and Wallenstein. Translated by S. T. C. (*Master-pieces of Foreign Literature, etc.*) London, 1866, 8vo.

Wallenstein. A dramatic poem. Part II. Piccolomini.—Part III. The Death of Wallenstein. [Translated by S. T. C.] (*Schiller. Complete Works . . . Edited . . . by C. J. Hempel, vol.* i.) Philadelphia, 1870, 8vo.

The Watchman . . . published by the author, S. T. C. 10 Nos. Bristol, 1796, 8vo.

VII.

BOOKS IN THE LIBRARY OF THE BRITISH MUSEUM CONTAINING MS. NOTES BY COLERIDGE.

Adam, T., *Rector of Wintringham.* —Private thoughts on religion, etc. York, 1795, 12mo,

Age. The Age. A poem, etc. London, 1829, 8vo.

Beaumont, F., and Fletcher, J.— Fifty Comedies and Tragedies, etc. London, 1679, fol.

Bible.—New Testament.—Revelation. — Appendix. De Equo Albo, etc. [By E. Swedenborg]. Londini, 1758, 4to.

Blanco White, J. M.—Practical and internal evidence against Catholicism, etc. London, 1825, 8vo.

Boyer, J. B. De.—Des Herrn Marquis d' Argens. Kabbalistische Briefe, etc. Danzig, 1773, etc., 8vo.

Dante Alighieri. [*Divina Commedia.*] The Vision. Translated

by H. F. Cary, etc. London, 1819, 8vo.

Desmoulins, A.—Histoire naturelle des races humaines, etc. Paris, 1826, 8vo.

Dubois, J. A.—Description of the character and customs of the people of India, etc. London, 1817, 4to.

Dyer, G.—Poems. London, 1800, 8vo.

——Poems, etc. London, 1801, 8vo.

England, Church of.—*Homilies.* Sermons or homilies of the United Church of England and Ireland, etc. London, 1815, 12mo.

Fichte, J. G.—Die Anweisung zum seeligen Leben, etc. Berlin, 1806, 8vo.

——Die Bestimmung des Menschen. Berlin, 1800, 8vo.

——Versuch einer Kritik aller Offenbarung, etc. Konigsberg, 1793, 8vo.

Fitzgibbon, J., *First Earl of Clare.* The speech of John Lord Baron Fitzgibbon, delivered in the House of Peers, March 13, 1793. Dublin [1793 ?], 8vo.

Godwin, W. — Thoughts occasioned by the perusal of Dr. Parr's Spital sermon. London, 1801, 8vo.

Grew, N.—Cosmologia Sacra, etc. London, 1701, fol.

Hegel, G. W. F.—Wissenschaft der Logik. Nürnberg, 1812, etc., 8vo.

Heinroth, J. C. F. A.—Lehrbuch der Anthropologie, etc. Leipzig, 1822, 8vo.

Herder J. G. von.—Briefe das Studium der Theologie betreffend, etc. Frankfurt, 1790, 8vo.

Herder, J. G. von.—Kalligone, etc. Leipzig, 1800, 8vo.

——Von der Auferstehung, als Glauben, Geschichte und Lehre. Frankfurt, 1794, 8vo.

Jahn, J.—The History of the Hebrew Commonwealth, etc. Oxford, 1829, 8vo.

Jurieu, P.—The History of the Council of Trent, etc. London, 1684, 8vo.

Kant, I.—Immanuel Kant's vermischte Schriften. Zweiter (-vierter) Band. Halle, 1799, etc,, 8vo.

——Sammlung einiger bisher unbekannt gebliebener kleiner Schriften, etc. Königsberg, 1800, 8vo.

——Anthropologie in pragmatischer Hinsicht abgefasst, etc. Königsberg, 1800, 8vo.

——I. Kant's Logik, etc. Königsberg, 1800, 8vo.

Coleridge's notes to this work are included in Kant's "Introduction to Logic," translated by T. K. Abbott, London, 1885.

——Die Metaphysik der Sitten. Königsberg, 1797, 8vo.

——Die Religion innerhalb der Grenzen der blossen Vernunft, etc. Königsberg, 1794, 8vo.

Lacunza, M. [*i.e.* Juan Josafat Ben-Ezra].—The coming of Messiah in glory and majesty, etc. London, 1827, 8vo.

Lloyd, C., *Poet.*—Nugæ Canoræ. Poems. Third edition, with additions [including a sonnet by S. T. C.]. London, 1819, 8vo.

Malthus, T. R.—An Essay on the Principles of Population, etc. London, 1803, 4to.

Mendelssohn, M.—Jerusalem, oder über religiöse Macht und Judenthum. Frankfurt, 1791, 8vo.

Mendelssohn, M.—Moses Mendelssohns Morgenstunden, etc. Frankfurt, 1790, 8vo.

Mesmer, F. A. — Mesmerismus, etc. Berlin, 1814, etc., 8vo.

Miller, John, *M.A., Fellow of Worcester College, Oxford.* Sermons intended to show a sober application of Scriptural principles to the realities of life, etc. London, 1830, 8vo.

Novalis.—Novalis Schriften, etc. Berlin, 1815, 8vo.

Oersted, H. C. — Ansicht der chemischen Naturgesetze durch die neueren Entdeckungen gewonnen, etc. Berlin, 1812, 8vo.

Oken, L.—Erste Ideen zur Theorie des Lichts, etc. Jena, 1808, 4to.

Omniana.—Omniana ; or Horae Otiosiores. London, 1812, 12mo.

Philalethes, A., *pseud.*—Observations upon Anthroposophia Theomagica, and Anima Magica Abscondita, etc. Parrhesia [London], 1650, 8vo.

——The second lash of Alazonomastix, etc. Cambridge, 1651, 8vo.

Sachs, H. — H. Sachsens sehr herrliche schöne und wahrhafte Gedicht, etc. Nürnberg, 1781, 8vo.

Schelling, F. W. J. Von.—Ideen zu einer Philosophie der Natur, etc. Landshut, 1803, 8vo.

Schelling, F. W. J. Von.—System des transscendentalen Idealismus. Tübingen, 1800, 8vo.

Schleiermacher, F. E. D.—Ueber den sogenannten ersten Brief des Paulos an den Timotheos, etc. Berlin, 1807, 8vo.

Scholz, J. M. A.—Commentatio de Golgothæ et Sanctissimi D. N. J. C. sepulcri situ. Bonnae, 1825, 4to.

Schubert, G. H. Von. Ansichten von der Nachtseite der Natur-wissenschaft. Dresden, 1808, 8vo.

——Die Symbolik des Traumes, etc. Bamberg, 1821, 8vo.

Shakespeare, W.—The Works of Shakespeare. With notes . . . by Mr. Theobald. 8 vols. London, 1773, 12mo.

Solger, C. W. F.—Philosophische Gespräche. Erste Sammlung. Berlin, 1817, 8vo.

Steffens, H.—Schriften, etc. 2 Bde. Breslau, 1821, 8vo.

——Beyträge zur innern Natur-geschichte der Erde. Erster Theil. Freyberg, 1801, 8vo.

——Caricaturen des Heiligsten. Leipzig, 1819, etc., 8vo.

——[Grundzüge der philoso-phischen Naturwissenschaft, etc.] Berlin [1806], 8vo.

——Ueber die Idee der Univer-sitäten, etc. Berlin, 1809, 8vo.

Stillingfleet, E., *Bishop of Wor-cester.* — Origines Sacræ, etc. London, 1675, 4to.

Tennemann, W. G.—Geschichte der Philosophie. Bde. 1-10. Leipzig, 1798, etc., 8vo.

Tennyson, C.—Sonnets and fugi-tive pieces. *MS. notes* [from notes by S. T. C.]. Cambridge, 1830, 8vo.

Tetens, J. N. — Philosophische Versuche über die menschliche Natur, etc. 2 Bde. Leipzig, 1777, 8vo.

Walckenaer, L. C. — Ludovici Caspari Valckenaeri diatribe de Aristobulo Judaeo, etc. Lug-duni Batavorum, 1806, 4to.

Waterland, D.—The importance of the Doctrine of the Holy Trinity asserted, etc. London, 1734, 8vo.

Willich, A. F. M.—Elements of the Critical Philosophy, etc. London, 1798, 8vo.

Wolff, C. Von, *Baron.*—Logic . . . Translated from the German, etc. London, 1770, 8vo.

VIII. APPENDIX.

BIOGRAPHY, CRITICISM, ETC.

Armstrong, Edmund J.—Essays and Sketches of Edmund J. Armstrong. London, 1877, 8vo.
Coleridge, pp. 38-96.

Bates, William.—The Maclise Por-trait Gallery of "Illustrious Literary Characters," with Me-moirs, etc. London, 1883, 8vo.
Samuel Taylor Coleridge, with portrait, pp. 178-185.

Bayne, Peter.—Essays in Bio-graphy and Criticism. Second series. Boston [U.S.], 1858, 8vo.
Samuel Taylor Coleridge, pp. 108-148.

Belfast, *Earl of.* — Poets and Poetry of the XIXth Century. A Course of Lectures by the Earl of Belfast. London, 1852, 8vo.
Lecture the first—Coleridge, Kirke White, Wordsworth, pp. 1-56.

Birks, T. R.—The Victory of Divine Goodness ; including notes on Coleridge's Confessions of an Inquiring Spirit, etc. London, 1867, 8vo.

Brandl, Alois. — Samuel Taylor Coleridge und die englische Romantik. Berlin, 1886, 8vo.

Brooke, S. A.—Theology in the English Poets : Cowper, Cole-ridge, Wordsworth, and Burns. London, 1874, 8vo.

——Brooke, S. A.—Theology in the English Poets. Second Edition. London, 1874, 8vo.

Caine, T. Hall.—Cobwebs of Criticism. London, 1883, 8vo.
Coleridge, pp. 54-87.

——Recollections of Dante Gabriel Rossetti. London, 1882, 8vo.
Coleridge, Wordsworth, etc., pp. 146-183.

Calvert (G. H.), Coleridge, Shelley, Goethe.—Biographic æsthetic studies. Boston [U.S.], [1880], 8vo.

Cambridge. — Conversations at Cambridge. [By R. A. Wilmott.] London, 1836, 8vo.
Samuel Taylor Coleridge at Trinity, with specimens of his Table Talk, pp. 1-4.

Carlyle, Thomas.—The Life of John Sterling. London, 1851, 8vo.
Coleridge, pp. 69-80.

Carlyon, Clement.—Early Years and Late Reflections. 4 vols. London, 1836-58, 12mo.
Carlyon was introduced to Coleridge at Göttingen in 1799, and much interesting matter relating to Coleridge's early life will be found in vols. i.-iii.

Chambers, Robert.—Cyclopædia of English Literature, etc. 2 vols. London, 1860, 8vo.
Samuel Taylor Coleridge, with portrait, vol. ii., pp. 291-303.

——Third Edition. London, 1876, 8vo.
Samuel Taylor Coleridge, vol. ii., pp. 68-79.

Chorley, Henry F.—The Authors of England. A Series of Medallion Portraits, etc. London, 1838, 4to.
Samuel Taylor Coleridge. pp 27-43.

——Another edition. London, 1861, 4to.

Clarke, Charles and Mary Cowden. —Recollections of Writers, etc. London, 1878, 8vo.
Samuel Taylor Coleridge, pp. 30-35 and 63-64.

——F. L.—Golden Friendships, etc. London, 1884, 8vo.
Lamb and Coleridge, pp. 160-183.

Cleveland, Charles Dexter.— English Literature of the Nineteenth Century. A new edition. Philadelphia, 1867, 8vo.
Samuel Taylor Coleridge, 1772-1834, pp. 216-230.

Cochrane, Robert.—The Treasury of Modern Biography, a Gallery of Literary Sketches, etc. Compiled and selected by Robert Cochrane. London, 1878, 8vo.
Samuel Taylor Coleridge, by Thomas de Quincey, pp. 129-164. Reprinted from Tait's Magazine, 1834.

Coleridge, Hartley.—Poems by H. C., with a memoir of his life by his brother [Derwent]. 2 vols. London, 1851, 8vo.
Contains many particulars relating to Samuel Taylor Coleridge.

——Samuel Taylor.—Coleridge on the Scripture. [Calcutta, 1851.] 8vo.
An essay on the argument of Coleridge's "Confessions of an Enquiring Spirit," reprinted from the Benares Magazine, 1851.

——Sara.—Memoir and Letters of S. C. 2 vols. London, 1873, 8vo.
Contains a number of important notices of Samuel Taylor Coleridge, especially in vol. i.

Collier, John Payne.—Collier, Coleridge, and Shakespeare A. review. By the author of "Literary Cookery." [i.e. A. E. Brae.] London, 1860, 8vo.

Collins, Mortimer.—Pen Sketches by a vanished hand, from the papers of the late Mortimer

Collins. Edited by Tom Taylor. 2 vols. London, 1879, 8vo.
Coleridge's Country, pp. 108-120. Appeared originally in *Belgravia* in 1870.

Colquhoun, John Campbell.—Scattered Leaves of Biography. London, 1864, 8vo.
Life of Samuel Taylor Coleridge, pp. 225-270.

Cotterill, H. B.—An Introduction to the Study of Poetry. London, 1882, 8vo.
Coleridge, pp. 179-207.

Cottle, Joseph.—Early Recollections, chiefly relating to the late S. T. Coleridge, during his residence in Bristol, etc. 2 vols. London, 1837 [-39], 8vo.
The copy in the British Museum is said to be the only one existing which has a second preface, 1839.

——Reminiscences of S. T. Coleridge and R. Southey. London, 1847, 8vo.

Courthope, William John.—The Liberal Movement in English Literature. London, 1885, 8vo.
Poetry, Music, and Painting: Coleridge and Keats, pp. 159-194.

Craik, George L.—A Manual of English Literature and of the History of the English Language. Ninth edition. London [1883], 8vo.
Coleridge, pp. 474-481.

——A Compendious History of English Literature, etc. 2 vols. London, 1861, 8vo.
Coleridge, vol. ii., pp. 456-473.

Davy, Sir Humphry.—Fragmentary Remains of Sir Humphry Davy. London, 1858, 8vo.
Contains a number of early letters of Samuel Taylor Coleridge.

Dennis, John.—Heroes of Literature.—English Poets. London, 1883, 8vo.
Samuel Taylor Coleridge, pp. 322-335.

De Quincey, Thomas.—De Quincey's Works. 16 vols. Edinburgh, 1862-71. 12mo.
Recollections of the Lakes and the Lake Poets, Coleridge, Wordsworth, and Southey, vol. ii., pp. 38-122; Coleridge and Opium-Eating, vol. xi., pp. 71-111.

Deshler, Charles D.—Afternoons with the Poets. New York, 1879, 4to.
Coleridge, pp. 215-220.

Detective. — Literary Cookery, with reference to matter attributed [by J. P. Collier] to Coleridge and Shakespeare. A letter addressed to *The Athenæum* [by one signing himself "A Detective," *i.e.*, A. E. Brae], etc. London, 1855, 8vo.
This publication was suppressed.

Devey, J.—A Comparative Estimate of Modern English Poets. London, 1873, 8vo.
The Lake Poets.—Coleridge, pp. 104-111.

Dowden, Edward. — Studies in Literature, 1789-1877. London, 1878, 8vo.
The Transcendental Movement and Literature, pp. 44-84.

England.—The Living Poets of England. 2 vols. Paris, 1827, 8vo.
S. T. Coleridge, vol. i., pp. 413-460.

Essay.—The relation of philosophy to theology, and of theology to religion. Reprinted from the Eclectic Review. Revised and enlarged. London, 1851. 16mo.
The head-title reads—" S. T. Coleridge, his philosophy and theology."

Essays.—Cambridge Essays, contributed by members of the University, 1856. London [1856], 8vo.
Coleridge, by F. J. A. Hort, pp. 292-351.

Fitzgerald, Percy.—Charles Lamb; his friends, his haunts, and his books. London, 1866, 8vo.

Fowler, Frank.—Last Gleanings, by the late Frank Fowler. London, 1864, 8vo.
Lectures.—Coleridge, pp. 167-200.

Fox, Caroline.—Memories of Old Friends, being extracts from the Journals and Letters of C. F., from 1835 to 1871. Edited by Horace N. Pym. London, 1882, 8vo.
Contains a number of interesting references to Samuel Taylor Coleridge.

Gilfillan, George.—A Gallery of Literary Portraits. Edinburgh, 1845, 8vo.
Samuel Taylor Coleridge,pp 265-288.

Gillman, James.—The Life of S. T. Coleridge. [With copious extracts from his works]. Vol. i. London, 1838, 8vo.
No more published.

Graham, J. Murray.—An historical view of Literature and Art in Great Britain. Second edition. London, 1872, 8vo.
Coleridge noticed, pp. 129-136.

Grattan, Thomas C. — Beaten Paths ; and those who trod them. 2 vols. London, 1862, 8vo.
"A Three Days' Tour with Coleridge and Wordsworth," vol. ii., pp. 107-145.

Green, Joseph Henry.—Spiritual Philosophy : founded on the teaching of S. T. C. Edited, with a Memoir of the Author's Life, by J. Simon. 2 vols. London, 1865, 8vo.

Grinsted, T. P.—Relics of Genius: Visits to the Last Homes of Poets, Painters, etc. With illustrations. London, 1859, 8vo.
Highgate.—Samuel Taylor Coleridge, pp. 191-193.

Hall, S. C.—A Book of Memories of Great Men and Women of the Age, from personal acquaintance. London, 1871, 4to.
Samuel Taylor Coleridge, pp. 27-48, with illustrations.

——Second edition. London, 1877, 4to.
Samuel Taylor Coleridge, pp. 27-48, with illustrations.

Hazlitt, William.—The Spirit of the Age ; or contemporary portraits. London, 1825, 8vo.
Mr. Coleridge, pp. 61-79.

——Memoirs of W. H., etc. 2 vols. London, 1867, 8vo.
Contains important references to S. T. Coleridge.

——Political Essays, with Sketches of Public Characters. London, 1819, 8vo.
Mr. Coleridge's Lay Sermon, pp. 118-124 ; Statesman's Manual, pp. 125-136.

——Literary Remains of the late W. H. 2 vols. London, 1836, 8vo.
Essay xix., vol. ii., pp. 361-396—My first acquaintance with poets.

—— W. Carew. — Offspring of Thought in Solitude. Modern Essays. London, 1884, 8vo.
"Coleridge Abroad," pp. 1-22.

Heraud, John Abraham.—An Oration on the death of S. T. Coleridge, delivered at the Russell Institution, etc. London, 1834, 8vo.

Hoffmann, Frederick A.—Poetry, its origin, nature and history : being a general sketch of poetic and dramatic literature. London, 1884, 8vo.
Coleridge, pp. 375-391.

Hogg, James.—The Poetic Mirror, or the Living Bards of Britain. [By James Hogg]. London, 1816, 8vo.
Contains two parodies on S. T. C. entitled "Isabelle" and "The Cherub."

Howitt, Will'am.—The Northern Heights of London; or, historical associations of Hampstead, Highgate, etc. London, 1869. 8vo.
Coleridge at Highgate, pp. 310-317.

——Homes and Haunts of the most Eminent British Poets. Third edition. London, 1857, 8vo.
Samuel Taylor Coleridge, pp. 393-418.

Jerdan, William.—Men I have known. London, 1866, 8vo.
Samuel Taylor Coleridge, pp. 119-131.

Johnson, Charles F.—Three Americans and Three Englishmen. Lectures read before the Students of Trinity College, Hartford. New York, 1886, 8vo.
Coleridge, pp. 41-87.

Lectures. — Lectures delivered before the Young Men's Christian Association in Exeter Hall. London, 1853, 8vo.
Coleridge and his followers, a lecture by the Rev. William M. Hetherington, Feb. 8th, 1853, pp. 407-448.

Le Grice, Charles V.—College Reminiscences of Coleridge. Reprinted from the *Gentleman's Magazine.* Penzance [1842], 8vo.

Leslie, Charles Robert.—Autobiographical Recollections. Edited by Tom Taylor. 2 vols. London, 1860, 8vo.
Contains much interesting matter relating to S. T. Coleridge.

Lester, John W.—Criticisms. Third edition. London, 1853, 8vo.
Coleridge, pp. 180-192.

Literary Speculum.—The L. S. 2 vols. London [1821-2], 12mo.
On the Poetry of Coleridge, with portrait, vol. ii., pp. 145-151.

Lowell, James R.—Democracy and other addresses. London, 1887, 8vo.

Coleridge. Address on unveiling the bust of Coleridge in Westminster Abbey, 7th May 1885, pp. 91-103.

Martineau, James.—Essays, philosophical and theological. New York, 1879, 8vo.
Personal influences on our present theology : Newman, Coleridge, Carlyle, vol. i., pp. 329-405.

Maurice, Frederick D.—Modern Philosophy; or, a Treatise of Moral and Metaphysical Philosophy, etc. London, 1862, 8vo.
Stuart, Bentham, Coleridge, pp. 635-672.

Meteyard, Eliza.—A Group of Englishmen (1795 to 1815), being records of the Wedgwoods and their Friends. London, 1871, 8vo.

Mill, John Stuart.—Dissertations and Discussions, political, philosophical, and historical, etc. 4 vols. London, 1859-75, 8vo.
Coleridge, vol. i., pp. 393-466. Reprinted from the *London and Westminster Review*, March 1840.

Moir, D. M.—Sketches of the poetical literature of the past half-century. Edinburgh, 1851, 8vo.
The origin, progress, and tenets of the Lake School, pp. 59-115.

Notes and Queries. — General Index to Notes and Queries. 5 Series. London, 1856-1880, 4to.
Numerous references to S. T. C.

Odds.—Odds and Ends. 2 vols. Edinburgh, 1857, 12mo.
No. 19, vol. ii., entitled " Bibliomania," contains " Marginalia—Coleridge on Southey, and on the ' Joan of Arc.'"

O'Hagan, Lord. — Occasional Papers and Addresses. London, 1884, 8vo.
Samuel Taylor Coleridge, pp. 200-240. [This paper was one of a series of " Afternoon Readings on Literature and Art" at the Museum, Stephen's Green, Dublin, in 1866.]

Oliphant, *Mrs.*—The Literary History of England, etc. 3 vols. London, 1882, 8vo.
S. T. Coleridge, vol. i., pp. 240-342.

Paris, John A.—The Life of Sir Humphry Davy. 2 vols. London, 1831, 8vo.
Contains many references to S. T. C.

Paul, C. Kegan.—William Godwin: his friends and contemporaries. 2 vols. London, 1876, 8vo.
Contains many references to and letters of S. T. Coleridge.

Phillips, Samuel.—Essays from "The Times." New edition. 2 vols. London, 1871, 8vo.
Reminiscences of Coleridge and Southey, by Joseph Cottle, vol. i., pp. 237-254.

Procter, Bryan Waller.—B. W. P. (Barry Cornwall). An Autobiographical Fragment, etc. [Edited by C. P., *i.e.* C. K. D. Patmore.] London, 1877, 8vo.
Wordsworth, Southey, Coleridge, pp. 137-148.

——Charles Lamb: a Memoir. By Barry Cornwall. London: 1866, 8vo.
Contains a number of notices of Samuel Taylor Coleridge.

Reed, Henry.—Lectures on the British Poets. 2 vols. Philadelphia, 1858, 8vo.
Coleridge, vol. ii., pp. 83-126.

Rhyme.—The Rime of the new-made Baccalere. [A parody of the "Ancient Mariner" of S. T. C.] Oxford, 1841, 8vo.

Richardson, David Lester.—Literary Chit-Chat, etc. Calcutta, 1848, 8vo.
Shelley, Keats, and Coleridge, pp. 271-281.

—— Literary Recreations; or essays, criticisms, and poems. London, 1852, 8vo.
Samuel Taylor Coleridge—born 1772, died 1834—pp. 538-541.

Rigg, James H.—Modern Anglican Theology; chapters on Coleridge, etc. London, 1857, 8vo.
——Second edition, revised and enlarged. London, 1859, 8vo.
——Third edition, revised. London [1880], 8vo.

Robberds, J. W.—A Memoir of the Life and Writings of the late William Taylor of Norwich, etc. 2 vols. London, 1843, 8vo.
Numerous references to S. T. C.

Robinson, Henry Crabb.—Diary, Reminiscences, and Correspondence of H. C. R. 3 vols. London, 1869, 8vo.
Contains a mass of interesting matter respecting S. T. Coleridge, and well indexed.

Rossetti, William Michael.—Lives of Famous Poets. London, 1878, 8vo.
Samuel Taylor Coleridge, pp. 237-255.

Royal Society of Literature.—Transactions of the Royal Society of Literature, vol. ix., 2nd series. London, 1870, 8vo.
Contains two papers by C. M. Ingleby, M.D., "On the Unpublished Manuscripts of S. T. C.," pp. 102-134; and "On some points connected with the Philosophy of Coleridge" (in reference to the preceding paper), pp. 396-429.

Seward, Anna.—Letters of A. S., written between the years 1784 and 1807. 6 vols. Edinburgh, 1811, 8vo.
Contains numerous references to S. T. Coleridge, in vols. iv., v., vi.

Shairp, J. C.—Studies in Poetry and Philosophy. Edinburgh, 1868, 8vo.
Coleridge, pp. 116-266.

Shedd, William G. T.—Literary Essays. New York, [1879], 8vo.
Coleridge as a philosopher and theologian, pp. 271-344.

Sketches.—Pen and Ink Sketches of Poets, Preachers, and Politicians. [By John Dix, otherwise J. D. Ross]. London, 1846, 8vo.
Reminiscences of Wordsworth, Coleridge, and Charles Lamb, pp. 122-139. A portrait (after Washington Allston) of Coleridge forms the frontispiece.

Southey, Robert.—The Life and Correspondence of R. S. Edited by C. C. Southey. 6 vols. London, 1849-50, 8vo.
Numerous references and letters to S. T. Coleridge.

——Selections from the Letters of R. S. Edited by John W. Warter. 4 vols. London, 1856, 8vo.
Contains numberless references to S. T. Coleridge.

Sterling, John.—Essays and Tales, by J. S. Collected and edited, with a memoir of his life, by Julius Charles Hare. 2 vols., London, 1848, 8vo.
On Coleridge's "Christabel" (from the *Athenæum* for 1828), pp. 101-110.

Stirling, James Hutchison.— Jerrold, Tennyson, and Macaulay, with other critical essays. Edinburgh, 1868, 8vo.
De Quincey and Coleridge upon Kant, pp. 172-224.

Sweetser, M. F.—Artist Biographies: Allston. Boston [U.S.], 1879, 12mo.
Contains biographical notes regarding W. Allston's acquaintance with S. T. Coleridge.

Swinburne, Algernon Charles.— Essays and Studies. London, 1875, 8vo.
Coleridge, pp. 259-275.

Talfourd, Thomas N. — Final Memorials of Charles Lamb, consisting of his letters, not before published, with sketches of some of his companions. 2 vols. London, 1848, 8vo.

Traill, H. D.—Coleridge, by H. D. Traill. (*English Men of Letters Series*). London, 1884, 8vo.

Tuckerman, Henry T.—Thoughts on the Poets. London, [1852], 8vo.
Coleridge, pp. 199-211.

Ward, Thomas H.—The English Poets, etc. Edited by T. H. Ward. 4 vols. London, 1883, 8vo.
Samuel Taylor Coleridge, by Walter H. Pater, vol. iv., pp. 102-154.

Whipple, Edwin P.—Essays and Reviews. Third edition. 2 vols. Boston, 1856, 8vo.
Vol. i.—English poets of the Nineteenth Century, — Coleridge, pp. 329-333 ; and Coleridge as a Philosophical Critic, (reprinted from the American Review, June 1846), pp. 405-421.

Wilson, *Professor.*—Essays, critical and imaginative. Edinburgh, 1866, 8vo.
Coleridge's Poetical Works (October 1834), pp. 293-343.

Wordsworth, Dorothy,—Recollections of a Tour made in Scotland, A.D., 1803. By D. W. Edited by J. C. Shairp. Edinburgh, 1874, 8vo.
Samuel Taylor Coleridge formed one of the party.

——, William.—Memoirs of W. W. By Christopher Wordsworth. 2 vols. London, 1851, 8vo.
Contains numerous important references to S. T. Coleridge.

MAGAZINE ARTICLES.

Coleridge, Samuel Taylor.—*Fraser's Magazine*, with portrait, vol. 8, 1833, p. 64.—*Colburn's*

Coleridge, Samuel Taylor.
New Monthly Magazine, vol.
42, 1834, pp. 55-63.—*Dublin
University Magazine,* vol. 6, July
1835, pp. 1-16, 250-267.—*North
American Review,* by G. B.
Cheever, vol. 40, April 1835,
pp. 299-351.—*American Quarterly Review,* vol. 19, 1836, pp.
1-28.—*Congregational Magazine,*
vol. 1, N.S., 1837, pp. 520-528.
—*Tait's Edinburgh Magazine,* by
T. De Quincey, vol. 1, N.S., pp.
509-520, 588-596, 685-690, vol. 2,
pp. 3-10.—*Christian Quarterly
Spectator,* by L. Withington,
vol. 6, pp. 617.—*London and
Westminster Review,* by J. S.
Mill, vol. 33, 1840, pp. 257-302.
—*Southern Literary Messenger,*
by H. T. Tuckerman, vol. 7,
1841, pp. 177-180.—*Princetown
Review,* by L. H. Atwater, vol.
20, April 1848, pp. 143-186.—
Hogg's Weekly Instructor, with
portrait, vol. 9, N.S., 1852, pp.
129-133 and 152-157.—*Methodist
Quarterly Review,* by D. Curry,
vol. 36, 1854, pp. 34-56.—
Evangelical Review, by M
Valentine, vol. 7, July 1855,
pp. 85-102.—*Bentley's Miscellany,* vol. 40, 1856, pp. 202-
220; same article, *Eclectic Magazine,* vol. 39, 1856, pp. 394-402.
—*Leisure Hour,* 1862, pp.
679-680.—*Art Journal* by S.
C. Hall, illustrated, vol. 4,
N.S., 1865, pp. 49-55; same
article, *Eclectic Magazine,*
June 1865, pp. 657-669.—*North
British Review,* vol. 43, 1865,
pp. 251-322; same article,
Littell's Living Age, vol.
88, 1866, pp. 81-99 and 161-
182.—*Blackwood's Edinburgh
Magazine,* vol. 110, Nov. 1871,

Coleridge, Samuel Taylor.
pp. 552-576; same article,
Eclectic Magazine, vol. 15,
N.S., 1872, pp. 138-157, and
Littell's Living Age, vol. 111,
1871, pp. 643-661.—*Canadian
Monthly,* vol. 13, 1878, pp.
362-365.—*National Magazine,*
vol. 1, p. 289, etc.—*Argosy,*
by Alice King, vol. 40, 1885,
pp. 116-122.—*Temple Bar,* by
Chas. J. Johnson, Sept. 1886,
pp. 35-54.—*La Revue Politique
et Littéraire,* by Léo Quesnel,
1877, pp. 219-224.—*London
Magazine,* vol. 7, 1823, pp.
85-90.

——Aids to Reflection. *New
York Review,* vol. 6, p. 477,
etc.; *Blackwood's Edinburgh
Magazine,* vol. 44, 1838, pp.
135-140.

——Ancient Mariner. *Journal
of Speculative Philosophy,* by
G. Garrigues, vol. 14, 1880,
pp. 327-338.

——And his American disciples.
Bibliotheca Sacra, by Rev.
Noah Porter, vol. 4, 1847, pp.
117-171.

——And Opium Eating. *Blackwood's Edinburgh Magazine,* by
T. De Quincey, vol. 57, 1845,
pp. 117-132.

——And Southey. *Edinburgh
Review,* vol. 87, 1848, pp.
368-392; same article, *Eclectic
Magazine,* vol. 14, 1848,
pp. 195-208; same article,
Littell's Living Age, vol. 17,
1848, pp. 310-320.—*Christian
Review,* vol. 15, 1850, pp. 321-
353.—*Examiner* [by W. Hazlitt],
April 6, 1817, p. 211.—*Examiner,* April 13, 1817, pp. 236, 237.

Coleridge, Samuel Taylor.
—— Anecdotes, Newspaper Writings and Letters of. *Gentleman's Magazine*, by D. Stuart, vol. 9, N.S., 1838, pp. 485-492 and 577-590 ; vol. 10, N.S., pp. 24-27 and 124-128.

—— ——Letters from H. N. Coleridge to Stuart in reference to preceding. *Gentleman's Magazine*, vol. 10, N.S., 1838, p. 22.

—— As a Poet. *American Presbyterian Review*, vol. 4, p. 80, etc. *Quarterly Review*, vol. 125, 1868, pp. 78-106 ; same article, *Littell's Living Age*, vol. 98, 1863, pp. 515-529.

—— As a Thinker. *Christian Review*, by R. Turnbull, vol. 19, 1854, pp. 321-342.

—— As a Poet and Man. *Atlantic Monthly*, by George P. Lathrop, vol. 45, 1880, pp. 483-498.

—— As a Poetical Critic. *Nation*, vol. 39, 1884, pp. 420-421.

—— Biographia Literaria. *Edinburgh Review*, by W. Hazlitt, vol. 28, 1817, pp. 488-515.— *Monthly Review*, vol. 88, 1819, pp.124-138.—*Blackwood's Edinburgh Magazine*, vol. 2, 1817, pp. 3-18, 285-288 ; vol. 3, 1818, pp. 653-657.

—— Christabel. *Edinburgh Review*, vol. 27, 1816, pp. 58-67.— *Monthly Review*, vol. 82, 1817, pp. 22-25.

—— Coleridgeiana. *Fraser's Magazine*, vol. 11, 1835, pp. 50-58.— *Littell's Museum of Foreign Literature*, vol. 26, pp. 359, etc.

—— Conciones ad Populum. *Analytical Review*, vol. 23, 1796, pp. 96-91.

—— Confessions of an Inquiring

Coleridge, Samuel Taylor.
Spirit. *Christian Observer*, vol. 50, 1850, pp. 234-250.

—— Cottle's Recollections of. *Congregational Magazine*, vol. 20, pp. 520, etc.—*Christian Observer*, vol. 37, 1837, pp. 594-611 and 632-638 ; vol. 59, 1859, pp. 374-385.—*Eclectic Review*, by J. Foster, vol. 2, N.S., 1837, pp. 137-164.—*Tait's Edinburgh Magazine*, vol. 4, N.S., 1837, pp. 341-348.

—— Country of. *Belgravia*, by Mortimer Collins, vol. 2, Second Series, 1870, pp. 197-203.

—— Death of. *Athenæum*, 1834, p. 574.

—— Early Recollections of. *Eclectic Review*, vol. 2, N.S., 1837, pp. 137-163.

—— Ethical Works of. *New York Review*, vol. 2, p. 96.— *American Quarterly Review*, vol. 19, 1856, pp. 1-28.—*London and Westminster Review*, by J. S. Mill, vol. 33, 1840, pp. 257-302.

—— Fall of Robespierre. *Analytical Review*, vol. 20, 1794, pp. 480-481.

—— Fears in Solitude. *Analytical Review*, vol. 28, 1798, pp. 590-592.

—— The Friend. *Eclectic Review*, by J. Foster, vol. 7, pt. 2, 1811, pp. 912-931.

—— Lamb's Last Words on. *New Monthly Magazine*, vol. 43, 1835, pp. 198-206.

—— Lay Sermon. *Edinburgh Review*, vol. 27, 1816, pp. 444-459.

—— Lectures of. *Tatler*, vol. 2, 1831, pp. 893, 894 and 897, 898.

—— Letters from. *Blackwood's*

Coleridge, Samuel Taylor.
Edinburgh Magazine, vol. 10, 1821, pp. 243-262.
——Letters from Germany. *New Monthly Magazine*, vol. 45, 1835, pp. 211-226.
——Letters of. *Western Literary Journal*, vol. 1, p. 198, etc.
——Letters to William Godwin. *Macmillan's Magazine*, vol. 9, 1864, pp. 524-536 ; same article, *Littell's Living Age*, vol. 81, 1864, pp. 275-285.
——Letters, Recollections, and Conversations of. *Tait's Edinburgh Magazine*, N.S., vol. 3, 1836, pp. 113-123.—*Monthly Review*, vol. 1, N.S., 1836, pp. 87-101—*Fraser's Literary Chronicle*, 1836, pp. 81-84, 101-105, 119-122.
——Letters to Matilda Betham. *Fraser's Magazine*, vol. 18, N.S., 1878, pp. 73-84.
——Life of (Gillman's). *Christian Observer*, vol. 59, 1859, pp. 308-318.—*Fraser's Magazine*, vol. 12, 1835, pp. 123-135.
——Life and Writings of. *British and Foreign Review*, vol. 8, 1839, pp. 414-451.—*American Whig Review*, by J. D. Whelpley, vol. 10, 1849, pp. 532-539 and 632-636.
——Literary Character of. *Christian Examiner*, by F. H. Hedge, vol. 14, 1833, pp. 109-129.
——Literary Life of. *Edinburgh Review*, by W. Hazlitt, vol. 28, 1817, pp. 488-515.
——Literary Remains of. *Quarterly Review*, by J. G. Lockhart, vol. 59, 1837, pp. 1-32.—*New York Review*, vol. 2, p. 96 ; and vol. 74, p. 403.—*Dublin University Magazine*, vol. 10, 1837, pp. 257-273.

Coleridge, Samuel Taylor.
——Lyrical Ballads.—*Analytical Review*, vol. 28, 1798, pp. 583-587.
——Marginalia. *Blackwood's Edinburgh Magazine*, by Helen Zimmern, vol. 131, 1882, pp. 107-125.—*North British Review*, vol. 11, 1864, pp. 79-84.
——Monologues. *Fraser's Magazine*, vol. 12, 1835, pp. 493-496 and 619-629.
——Obituary Notice. *Gentleman's Magazine*, vol. 2, N.S., 1834, pp. 544-549.
——Overlooked poem [The Volunteer Stripling]. *Gentleman's Magazine*, vol. 29, 1848, p. 160.
——Papers (Essays). *Fraser's Literary Chronicle*, 1836, pp. 184, 185, 201, 202, 217, 218, 232, 233, 248, 249.
——Personal influences on our present Theology : Newman, Coleridge, Carlyle. By J. Martineau. *National Review*, vol. 3, 1856, pp. 449-494.
——Personal Memories of. *Atlantic Monthly*, by S. C. and A. F. Hall, vol. 15, 1865, pp. 213-221.
——Philosophy of. *Fraser's Magazine*, vol. 5, 1832, pp. 585-597.
——Philosophy, and Theology of. *Eclectic Review*, N.S., vol. 1, 1851, pp. 1-22.
——Philosophy and Christianity. *Theological and Literary Journal*, by D. N. Lord, vol. 1, 1849, pp. 631-669.
——Plagiarisms of. *Blackwood's Edinburgh Magazine*, vol. 47, 1840, pp. 287-299.

Coleridge, Samuel Taylor,
——Poems on various subjects. *Analytical Review*, vol. 23, 1796, pp. 610-612.—*Monthly Review*, vol. 20, 1796, pp. 194-199.

——A Poetical Sphinx. *Victoria Magazine*, vol. 13, 1869, pp. 26-40.

——Poetical Works of. *Blackwood's Edinburgh Magazine*, vol. 6, 1819, pp. 1-12 ; vol. 36, 1834, pp. 542-570.—*Westminster Review*, vol. 12, 1829, pp. 1-31.—*Museum of Foreign Literature*, vol. 25, p. 560.—*North American Review*, by R. C. Watherston, vol. 39, 1834, pp.437-458.—*Quarterly Review*, by J. G. Lockhart, vol. 52, 1834, pp. 1-38.—*Etonian*, by Gerard Montgomery, vol. 1, 1821, pp. 307-318.

——Poetry, Music, and Painting : Coleridge and Keats. *National Review*, by W. J. Courthope, vol. 5, 1885, pp. 504-518.

——Recollections of. *Southern Literary Messenger*, vol. 2, 1836, pp. 451-453.—*North American Review*, by C. E. Norton, vol. 65, pp. 401-440.

——Reminiscences of. *Fraser's Magazine*, vol. 10, 1834, pp. 379-403.—*Christian Observer*, vol. 45, 1845, pp. 257-263.

——Remorse. *Christian Observer*, vol. 12, 1813, pp. 228-238.—*Quarterly Review*, vol. 11, 1814, pp. 177-190.—*London Magazine*, vol. 1, 1820, pp. 436, etc.

——Science and Logic. *Fraser's Magazine*, vol. 12, 1835, pp. 619-629.

——Sibylline Leaves. *Monthly Review*, vol. 88, 1819, pp. 24-38.

Coleridge, Samuel Taylor.
——Sketch of. *Tait's Edinburgh Magazine*, by T. De Quincey, vol. 6, N.S., 1839, pp. 513-517.

——Sketch of a Conversation between him and Kenyon. *Academy*, contributed by R. Browning, August 15, 1885, p. 105.

——Sonnet to Miss Barbour. *Athenæum*, May 3, 1884.

——Table Talk. *Quarterly Review*, by J. G. Lockhart, vol. 53, 1835, pp. 79-103.—*Edinburgh Review*, vol. 61, 1835, pp. 129-153.—*Christian Examiner*, by G. Putnam, vol. 19, 1836, pp. 204-215.—*Westminster Review*, by T. P. Thompson, vol. 22, 1835, pp. 531-537.—*Museum of Foreign Literature*, vol. 26, p. 442—*Dublin University Magazine*, vol. 6, 1835, pp. 1-16.—*American Monthly Magazine*, vol. 5, 1835, pp. 454-457.—*Monthly Review*, vol. 2, N.S., 1835, pp. 250-261.—*Fraser's Magazine*, vol. 12, 1835, pp. 123-135.

——Theology of. *Christian Observer*, vol. 59, 1859, pp. 634-639.

——The Three Graves (The Friend). *Monthly Mirror*,vol. 8, N.S., 1810, pp. 26-31, 98-105, 186-196.

——Two Round Spaces on the Tombstone. *Fraser's Magazine*, vol. 7, 1833, pp. 175-177, 367, 620-21.

——Unitarianism of. *Christian Reformer*, vol. 1, Second Series. 1834, pp. 837-840.

——Unpublished Letters of. *Lippincott's Magazine*, by G. M. Towle, vol. 13, 1874, pp. 697-710.—*Christian Observer*, vol.

Coleridge, Samuel Taylor.
45, 1845, pp. 81, 82, and 585-589.—*Westminster Review*, vol.
93, 1870, pp. 341-364; and vol.
94, pp. 1-24.
——Will of. *Gentleman's Magazine*, vol. 2, N.S., 1834, pp. 661-663.
——With Socinians and Atheists.

Coleridge, Samuel Taylor.
Congregational Magazine, vol. 18, 1835, pp. 486-490.
——Works of. *London Weekly Review*, vol. 2, 1828, pp. 369, 370.—*American Church Review*, by A. N. Littlejohn, vol. 6, p. 480.—*Westminster Review*, vol. 29, N.S., 1866, pp. 106-132.

CHRONOLOGICAL LIST OF WORKS.

UNWIN BROTHERS,

THE GRESHAM PRESS,

CHILWORTH AND LONDON